Scott

Science

The Diamond Edition

PEARSON
Scott
Foresman

Editorial Offices: Glenview, Illinois • Parsippany, New Jersey • New York, New York
Sales Offices: Boston, Massachusetts • Duluth, Georgia • Glenview, Illinois •
Coppell, Texas • Sacramento, California • Mesa, Arizona
www.pearsonsuccessnet.com

Series Authors

Dr. Timothy Cooney
Professor of Earth Science and Science Education
University of Northern Iowa (UNI)
Cedar Falls, Iowa

Dr. Jim Cummins
Professor
Department of Curriculum, Teaching, and Learning
The University of Toronto
Toronto, Canada

Dr. James Flood
Distinguished Professor of Literacy and Language
School of Teacher Education
San Diego State University
San Diego, California

Barbara Kay Foots, M.Ed.
Science Education Consultant
Houston, Texas

Dr. M. Jenice Goldston
Associate Professor of Science Education
Department of Elementary Education Programs
University of Alabama
Tuscaloosa, Alabama

Dr. Shirley Gholston Key
Associate Professor of Science Education
Instruction and Curriculum Leadership Department
College of Education
University of Memphis
Memphis, Tennessee

Dr. Diane Lapp
Distinguished Professor of Reading and Language Arts in Teacher Education
San Diego State University
San Diego, California

Sheryl A. Mercier
Classroom Teacher
Dunlap Elementary School
Dunlap, California

Karen L. Ostlund, Ph.D.
UTeach Specialist
College of Natural Sciences
The University of Texas at Austin
Austin, Texas

Dr. Nancy Romance
Professor of Science Education & Principal Investigator
NSF/IERI Science IDEAS Project
Charles E. Schmidt College of Science
Florida Atlantic University
Boca Raton, Florida

Dr. William Tate
Chair and Professor of Education and Applied Statistics
Department of Education
Washington University
St. Louis, Missouri

Dr. Kathryn C. Thornton
Former NASA Astronaut Professor
School of Engineering and Applied Science
University of Virginia
Charlottesville, Virginia

Dr. Leon Ukens
Professor Emeritus
Department of Physics, Astronomy, and Geosciences
Towson University
Towson, Maryland

Steve Weinberg
Consultant
Connecticut Center for Advanced Technology
East Hartford, Connecticut

ISBN: 978-0-328-28960-8; 0-328-28960-4 (SVE); 978-0-328-30442-4;
0-328-30442-5 (A); 978-0-328-30443-1; 0-328-30443-3 (B); 978-0-328-30444-8;
0-328-30444-1 (C); 978-0-328-30445-5; 0-328-30445-X (D)

Consulting Author

Dr. Michael P. Klentschy
Superintendent
El Centro Elementary School District
El Centro, California

Science Content Consultants

Dr. Frederick W. Taylor
Senior Research Scientist
Institute for Geophysics
Jackson School of Geosciences
The University of Texas at Austin
Austin, Texas

Dr. Ruth E. Buskirk
Senior Lecturer
School of Biological Sciences
The University of Texas at Austin
Austin, Texas

Dr. Cliff Frohlich
Senior Research Scientist
Institute for Geophysics
Jackson School of Geosciences
The University of Texas at Austin
Austin, Texas

Brad Armosky
McDonald Observatory
The University of Texas at Austin
Austin, Texas

NASA Content Consultants

Adena Williams Loston, Ph.D.
Chief Education Officer
Office of the Chief Education Officer

Clifford W. Houston, Ph.D.
Deputy Chief Education Officer for Education Programs
Office of the Chief Education Officer

Frank C. Owens
Senior Policy Advisor
Office of the Chief Education Officer

Deborah Brown Biggs
Manager, Education Flight Projects Office
Space Operations Mission Directorate Education Lead

Erika G. Vick
NASA Liaison to Pearson Scott Foresman
Education Flight Projects Office

William E. Anderson
Partnership Manager for Education
Aeronautics Research Mission Directorate

Anita Krishnamurthi
Program Planning Specialist
Space Science Education and Outreach Program

Bonnie J. McClain
Chief of Education
Exploration Systems Mission Directorate

Diane Clayton, Ph.D.
Program Scientist
Earth Science Education

Deborah Rivera
Strategic Alliances Manager
Office of Public Affairs
NASA Headquarters

Douglas D. Peterson
Public Affairs Officer, Astronaut Office
Office of Public Affairs
NASA Johnson Space Center

Nicole Cloutier
Public Affairs Officer, Astronaut Office
Office of Public Affairs
NASA Johnson Space Center

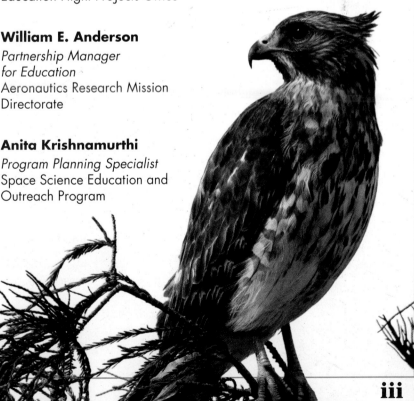

Reviewers

Dr. Maria Aida Alanis
Administrator
Austin ISD
Austin Texas

Melissa Barba
Teacher
Wesley Mathews Elementary
Miami, Florida

Dr. Marcelline Barron
Supervisor/K-12 Math
and Science
Fairfield Public Schools
Fairfield, Connecticut

Jane Bates
Teacher
Hickory Flat Elementary
Canton, Georgia

Denise Bizjack
Teacher
Dr. N. H. Jones
Elementary
Ocala, Florida

Latanya D. Bragg
Teacher
Davis Magnet School
Jackson, Mississippi

Richard Burton
Teacher
George Buck Elementary
School 94
Indianapolis, Indiana

Dawn Cabrera
Teacher
E.W.F. Stirrup School
Miami, Florida

Barbara Calabro
Teacher
Compass Rose Foundation
Ft. Myers, Florida

Lucille Calvin
Teacher
Weddington Math &
Science School
Greenville, Mississippi

Patricia Carmichael
Teacher
Teasley Middle School
Canton, Georgia

Martha Cohn
Teacher
An Wang Middle School
Lowell, Massachusetts

Stu Danzinger
Supervisor
Community Consolidated
School District 59
Arlington Heights, Illinois

Esther Draper
Supervisor/Science Specialist
Belair Math Science
Magnet School
Pine Bluff, Arkansas

Sue Esser
Teacher
Loretto Elementary
Jacksonville, Florida

Dr. Richard Fairman
Teacher
Antioch University
Yellow Springs, Ohio

Joan Goldfarb
Teacher
Indialantic Elementary
Indialantic, Florida

Deborah Gomes
Teacher
A J Gomes Elementary
New Bedford, Massachusetts

Sandy Hobart
Teacher
Mims Elementary
Mims, Florida

Tom Hocker
Teacher/Science Coach
Boston Latin Academy
Dorchester, Massachusetts

Shelley Jaques
Science Supervisor
Moore Public Schools
Moore, Oklahoma

Marguerite W. Jones
Teacher
Spearman Elementary
Piedmont, South Carolina

Kelly Kenney
Teacher
Kansas City Missouri
School District
Kansas City, Missouri

Carol Kilbane
Teacher
Riverside Elementary School
Wichita, Kansas

Robert Kolenda
Teacher
Neshaminy School District
Langhorne, Pennsylvania

Karen Lynn Kruse
Teacher
St. Paul the Apostle
Yonkers, New York

Elizabeth Loures
Teacher
Point Fermin
Elementary School
San Pedro, California

Susan MacDougall
Teacher
Brick Community Primary
Learning Center
Brick, New Jersey

Jack Marine
Teacher
Raising Horizons Quest
Charter School
Philadelphia, Pennsylvania

Nicola Micozzi Jr.
Science Coordinator
Plymouth Public Schools
Plymouth, Massachusetts

Paula Monteiro
Teacher
A J Gomes Elementary
New Bedford, Massachusetts

Tracy Newallis
Teacher
Taper Avenue Elementary
San Pedro, California

Dr. Eugene Nicolo
Supervisor, Science K-12
Moorestown School District
Moorestown, New Jersey

Jeffrey Pastrak
School District of Philadelphia
Philadelphia, Pennsylvania

Helen Pedigo
Teacher
Mt. Carmel Elementary
Huntsville Alabama

Becky Peltonen
Teacher
Patterson Elementary School
Panama City, Florida

Sherri Pensler
Teacher/ESOL
Claude Pepper Elementary
Miami, Florida

Virginia Rogliano
Teacher
Bridgeview Elementary
South Charleston,
West Virginia

Debbie Sanders
Teacher
Thunderbolt Elementary
Orange Park, Florida

Grethel Santamarina
Teacher
E.W.F. Stirrup School
Miami, Florida

Migdalia Schneider
Teacher/Bilingual
Lindell School
Long Beach, New York

Susan Shelly
Teacher
Bonita Springs Elementary
Bonita Springs, Florida

Peggy Terry
Teacher
Madison District 151
South Holland, Illinois

Jane M. Thompson
Teacher
Emma Ward Elementary
Lawrenceburg, Kentucky

Martha Todd
Teacher
W. H. Rhodes Elementary
Milton, Florida

Renee Williams
Teacher
Central Elementary
Bloomfield, New Mexico

Myra Wood
Teacher
Madison Street Academy
Ocala, Florida

Marion Zampa
Teacher
Shawnee Mission
School District
Overland Park, Kansas

Science

See learning in a whole new light

Unit A Life Science

What are some ways to classify living things?

Chapter 1 • Classifying Plants and Animals

Chapter 2 • Energy from Plants

What features
help plants
make their
own food and
reproduce?

Unit A Life Science

How do organisms interact with each other and with their environment?

How do changes in ecosystems affect our world?

Chapter 5 • Systems of the Human Body

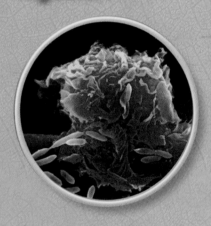

How do the body's smallest and largest parts work together?

Unit B Earth Science

How does Earth's water affect weather?

Chapter 6 • Water Cycle and Weather

Chapter 7 • Hurricanes and Tornadoes

How do storms affect Earth's air, water, land, and living things?

Unit B Earth Science

How can rocks tell us about Earth's past, present, and future?

How is Earth's surface shaped and reshaped?

Chapter 8 • Minerals and Rocks

Chapter 9 • Changes to Earth's Surface

Chapter 10 • Using Natural Resources

How can living things always have the natural resources they need?

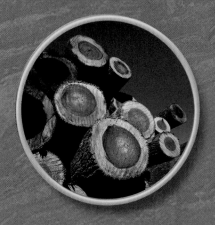

Unit C · Physical Science

Chapter 11 • Properties of Matter

How can matter be compared, measured, and combined?

Chapter 12 • Heat

How does heat energy move from one object to another?

Chapter 13 • Electricity and Magnetism

What are some ways that energy can be changed from one type to another?

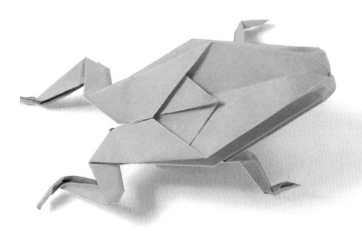

Unit C Physical Science

How do sound and light travel?

What causes motion and how does it affect us?

Chapter 14 • Sound and Light

Chapter 15 • Objects in Motion

Chapter 16 • Simple Machines

How do simple machines make work easier?

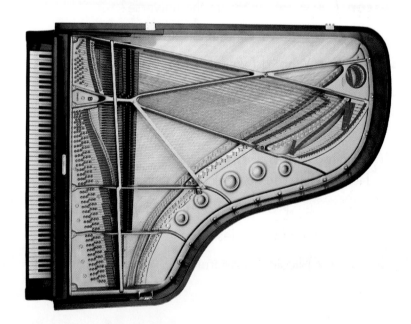

Unit D Space and Technology

How are cycles on Earth affected by the Sun and the Moon?

How is Earth different from other planets in our solar system?

Chapter 19 • Effects of Technology

How do the
devices and
products of
technology
affect the
way we live?

How to Read Science

A page like the one below is found near the beginning of each chapter. It shows you how to use a reading skill that will help you understand what you read.

Before Reading

Before you read the chapter, read the Build Background page and think about how to answer the question. Recall what you already know as you answer the question. Work with a partner to make a list of what you already know. Then read the How to Read Science page.

Target Reading Skill
Each page has one target reading skill. The reading skill corresponds with a process skill in the Directed Inquiry activity on the facing page. The reading skill will be useful as you read science.

Real-World Connection
Each page has an example of something you might read. It also connects with the Directed Inquiry activity.

Graphic Organizer
A useful strategy for understanding anything you read is to make a graphic organizer. A graphic organizer can help you think about the information and how parts of it relate to each other. Each reading skill has a graphic organizer.

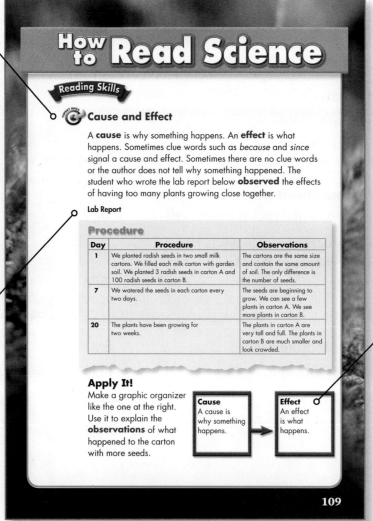

How to Read Science

Reading Skills

Cause and Effect

A **cause** is why something happens. An **effect** is what happens. Sometimes clue words such as *because* and *since* signal a cause and effect. Sometimes there are no clue words or the author does not tell why something happened. The student who wrote the lab report below **observed** the effects of having too many plants growing close together.

Lab Report

Procedure

Day	Procedure	Observations
1	We planted radish seeds in two small milk cartons. We filled each milk carton with garden soil. We planted 3 radish seeds in carton A and 100 radish seeds in carton B.	The cartons are the same size and contain the same amount of soil. The only difference is the number of seeds.
7	We watered the seeds in each carton every two days.	The seeds are beginning to grow. We can see a few plants in carton A. We see more plants in carton B.
20	The plants have been growing for two weeks.	The plants in carton A are very tall and full. The plants in carton B are much smaller and look crowded.

Apply It!
Make a graphic organizer like the one at the right. Use it to explain the **observations** of what happened to the carton with more seeds.

Cause		Effect
A cause is why something happens.	→	An effect is what happens.

109

Species Then and Now

Fossils show us that life on Earth has not always been the same as it is now. Over long periods of time, changes in the environment have caused species to change or adapt as well. Scientists can compare fossils of organisms that lived long ago with organisms that are alive today.

Woolly mammoths lived long ago. They have since become extinct, but many are preserved as fossils. Some mammoths have been frozen solid. Scientists compare these frozen mammoths with modern elephants. They both have large tusks and long noses. Their skeletons are also very much alike. Both the woolly mammoth and modern elephants are classified in the same family.

Fossils can also tell us about the environment long ago. Sometimes fossils of marine creatures are found in dry climates. This tells scientists that long ago shallow seas must have covered the area where the fossils were found.

In ancient times, many kinds of sea lilies filled the oceans. Many sea lilies have been preserved as fossils.

1. √ **Checkpoint** When are species considered threatened?

2. ◑ **Cause and Effect** Why do organisms become extinct?

Today only a few species of sea lilies remain. These flower-like animals attach themselves to the ocean floor.

121

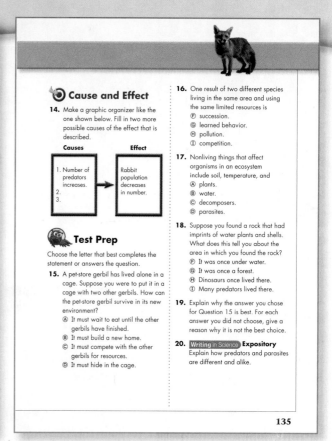

◑ Cause and Effect

14. Make a graphic organizer like the one shown below. Fill in two more possible causes of the effect that is described.

Causes → **Effect**

1. Number of predators increases.
2.
3.

→ Rabbit population decreases in number.

🦉 Test Prep

Choose the letter that best completes the statement or answers the question.

15. A pet-store gerbil has lived alone in a cage. Suppose you were to put it in a cage with two other gerbils. How can the pet-store gerbil survive in its new environment?
 Ⓐ It must wait to eat until the other gerbils have finished.
 Ⓑ It must build a new home.
 Ⓒ It must compete with the other gerbils for resources.
 Ⓓ It must hide in the cage.

16. One result of two different species living in the same area and using the same limited resources is
 Ⓕ succession.
 Ⓖ learned behavior.
 Ⓗ pollution.
 Ⓘ competition.

17. Nonliving things that affect organisms in an ecosystem include soil, temperature, and
 Ⓐ plants.
 Ⓑ water.
 Ⓒ decomposers.
 Ⓓ parasites.

18. Suppose you found a rock that had imprints of water plants and shells. What does this tell you about the area in which you found the rock?
 Ⓕ It was once under water.
 Ⓖ It was once a forest.
 Ⓗ Dinosaurs once lived there.
 Ⓘ Many predators lived there.

19. Explain why the answer you chose for Question 15 is best. For each answer you did not choose, give a reason why it is not the best choice.

20. Writing in Science **Expository** Explain how predators and parasites are different and alike.

135

◑ During Reading

As you read the lesson, use the checkpoint to check your understanding. Some checkpoints ask you to use the reading target skill.

◑ After Reading

After you have read the chapter, think about what you found out. Exchange ideas with a partner. Compare the list you made before you read the chapter with what you learned by reading it. Answer the questions in the Chapter Review. One question uses the reading target skill.

Graphic Organizers

These are the target reading skills and graphic organizers that appear in this book.

☐→☐ Cause and Effect

⬭ Compare and Contrast

Sequence

☐→☐ Predict

Draw Conclusions

Summarize

Main Idea and Details

Science Process Skills

Investigating the Everglades

Scientists use process skills when they investigate places or events. You will use these skills when you do the activities in this book. Which process skills might scientists use when they investigate the animals and plants of the Everglades?

Observe
A scientist investigating the Everglades observes many things. You use your senses too to find out about other objects, events, or living things.

Classify
Scientists classify living things in the Everglades according to their characteristics. When you classify, you arrange or sort objects, events, or living things.

Estimate and Measure
Scientists might estimate the size of a tree in the Everglades. When they estimate, they tell what they think an object's size, mass, or temperature will measure. Then they measure these factors in units.

Infer
During an investigation, scientists infer what they think is happening, based on what they already know.

Predict
Before they go into the Everglades, scientists tell what they think they will find.

Make and Use Models
Scientists might make and use models, such as maps, to help plan where to go during an investigation.

Make Operational Definitions
When scientists make operational definitions, they describe objects or events based on their experiences.

Science Process Skills

Form Questions and Hypotheses

Think of a statement that you can test to solve a problem or answer a question about the animals you see in the Everglades.

If you were a scientist, you might explore further into the Everglades. What questions might you have about the living things you see? How would you use process skills in your investigation?

Collect Data

Scientists collect data from their observations in the Everglades. They put the data into charts or tables.

Interpret Data

Scientists use the information they collected to solve problems or answer questions.

Investigate and Experiment
As the scientists explore the Everglades, they investigate and experiment to test a hypothesis.

Identify and Control Variables
As scientsts perform an experiment, they identify and control the variables so that they test only one thing at a time.

Communicate
Scientists use words, pictures, charts, and graphs to share information about their investigation.

Using Scientific Methods for Science Inquiry

Scientists use scientific methods as they work. Scientific methods are organized ways to answer questions and solve problems. Scientific methods include the steps shown here. Scientists might not use all the steps. They might not use the steps in this order. You will use scientific methods when you do the **Full Inquiry** activity at the end of each unit. You also will use scientific methods when you do Science Fair Projects.

Ask a question.
You might have a question about something you observe.

What material is best for keeping heat in water?

State your hypothesis.
A hypothesis is a possible answer to your question.

If I wrap the jar in fake fur, then the water will stay warmer longer.

Identify and control variables.
Variables are things that can change. For a fair test, you choose just one variable to change. Keep all other variables the same.

Test other materials. Put the same amount of warm water in other jars that are the same type, size, and shape.

Test your hypothesis.

Make a plan to test your hypothesis. Collect materials and tools. Then follow your plan.

Collect and record your data.

Keep good records of what you do and find out. Use tables and pictures to help.

Interpret your data.

Organize your notes and records to make them clear. Make diagrams, charts, or graphs to help.

State your conclusion.

Your conclusion is a decision you make based on your data. Communicate what you found out. Tell whether or not your data supported your hypothesis.

Fake fur did the best job of keeping the water warm.

Go further.

Use what you learn. Think of new questions to test or better ways to do a test.

Ask a Question

State Your Hypothesis

Identify and Control Variables

Test Your Hypothesis

Collect and Record Your Data

Interpret Your Data

State Your Conclusion

Go Further

Science Tools

Scientists use many different kinds of tools. Tools can make objects appear larger. They can help you measure volume, temperature, length, distance, and mass. Tools can help you figure out amounts and analyze your data. Tools can also help you find the latest scientific information.

You can use a **telescope** to help you see the stars. Some telescopes have special mirrors that gather lots of light and magnify things that are very far away, such as stars and planets.

You can use a **magnifying lens** or **hand lens** to make objects appear larger and to show more detail than you could see with just your eyes. A **hand lens** doesn't enlarge things as much as microscopes do, but it is easier to carry on a field trip.

A **metric tape** can be used like a meterstick or ruler to measure length, but it is flexible to measure around objects.

Pictures taken with a **camera** record what something looks like. You can compare pictures of the same object to show how the object might have changed over time.

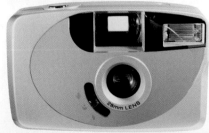

Microscopes use several lenses to make objects appear much larger, so you can see more detail.

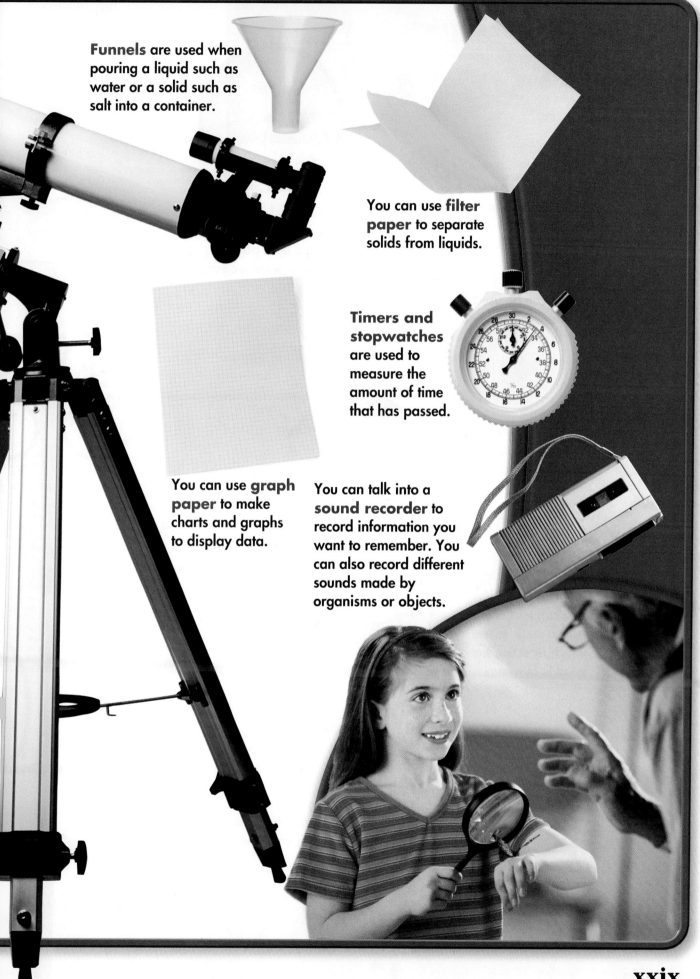

Funnels are used when pouring a liquid such as water or a solid such as salt into a container.

You can use **filter paper** to separate solids from liquids.

Timers and stopwatches are used to measure the amount of time that has passed.

You can use **graph paper** to make charts and graphs to display data.

You can talk into a **sound recorder** to record information you want to remember. You can also record different sounds made by organisms or objects.

Science Tools

You use a **thermometer** to measure temperature. Many thermometers have both Fahrenheit and Celsius scales. Scientists usually use only the Celsius scale. Thermometers also can be used to help measure a gain or loss of energy.

Scientists use **barometers** to measure air pressure, which can be a good indicator of weather patterns.

A **weather vane** is used to determine wind direction.

You can look at a **wind sock** to see which direction the wind is blowing.

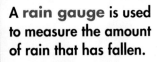

A **rain gauge** is used to measure the amount of rain that has fallen.

Terminals are parts of batteries or other devices to which wires are attached to form an electric circuit.

A **multimeter** can measure several characteristics of electricity.

You can use **computers** in many ways, such as to help collect, record, and analyze data.

Calculators make analyzing data easier and faster.

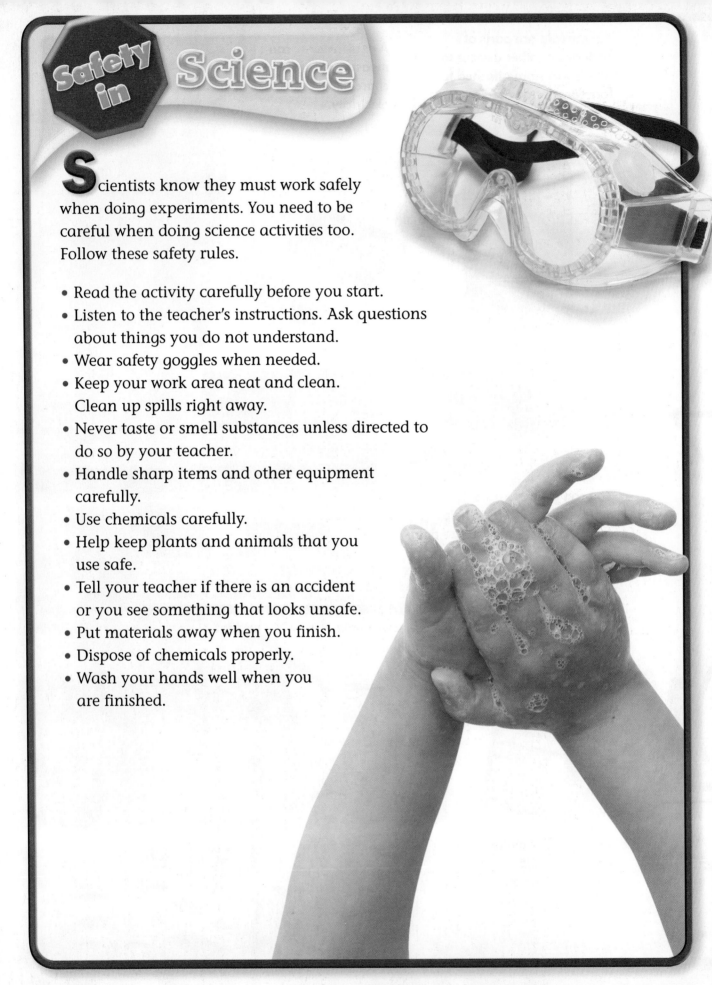

Safety in Science

Scientists know they must work safely when doing experiments. You need to be careful when doing science activities too. Follow these safety rules.

- Read the activity carefully before you start.
- Listen to the teacher's instructions. Ask questions about things you do not understand.
- Wear safety goggles when needed.
- Keep your work area neat and clean. Clean up spills right away.
- Never taste or smell substances unless directed to do so by your teacher.
- Handle sharp items and other equipment carefully.
- Use chemicals carefully.
- Help keep plants and animals that you use safe.
- Tell your teacher if there is an accident or you see something that looks unsafe.
- Put materials away when you finish.
- Dispose of chemicals properly.
- Wash your hands well when you are finished.

Chapter 11

Properties of Matter

You Will Discover

- what makes up matter.
- that all matter has mass, weight, volume, and density.
- how the properties of substances change.
- ways that substances combine to form new substances.

online
Student Edition
pearsonsuccessnet.com

How can matter be compared, measured, and combined?

physical change

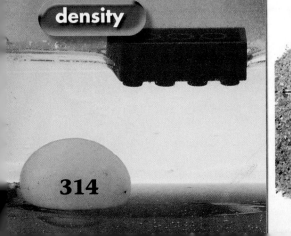

density

314

mixture

Chapter 11 Vocabulary

chemical change

solvent

solute

solution

solubility

315

Explore What properties cause liquids to form layers?

Materials

corn syrup

dishwashing liquid

water (with red food coloring)

corn oil

cup

small paper clip
tiny piece of Styrofoam®
piece of rubber band

What to Do

1 Pour in each liquid in the order they are listed in the materials section.

2 **Observe** that the liquids form layers.

3 Gently drop in a small paper clip. Watch until it stops sinking. Next, drop in a piece of Styrofoam.® Wait until it stops. Then drop in a piece of rubber band.

Because of their different properties, these liquids can form layers.

A liquid with a higher density will sink under a liquid with a lower density.

Explain Your Results

1. **Infer** Based on your **observations**, which liquid has the highest density? the lowest density? How do you know?

2. Which object has the highest density? the lowest density? How do you know?

Process Skills

You make **inferences** when you develop ideas based on **observations.**

Compare and Contrast

Comparing and contrasting information helps you understand some kinds of writing. We compare when we say how things are alike and contrast when we say how they are different.

- Writers use clue words to signal likenesses and differences. The most common clue word for likenesses is *like*.
- Clue words such as *yet, but,* and *however* signal differences.

In the lab report below, the student made **observations** that compare and contrast the water and ice in the activity.

Lab Report

Day	Action	Observations
1	We put water in the freezer.	Water was liquid.
2	The water was frozen into ice. We put the ice into a glass of water.	The ice floated on the water.

Ice is the same substance as water. But the temperature of ice is lower. That's why it's a solid instead of a liquid. So we were surprised that the ice floated on the water. Later, the ice was beginning to melt. It was smaller than before but still floated on the water.

Apply It!

Use a graphic organizer like the one shown. Write **observations** that **compare and contrast** ice and water.

Alike

Different

You Are There!

You hear the liquid water rushing beneath the boat. You glance down at the deck. You notice the puddles from yesterday's rain have disappeared. The water has evaporated into the air around you. As the boat approaches the iceberg, you reach out to feel a solid wall of water. How does the water that surrounds you change form?

AudioText

Lesson 1

What is matter?

All forms of matter are made up of tiny particles that are too small to see. The way these particles are arranged and move determines whether the matter is a solid, liquid, or gas.

Properties of Matter

Like ice, water, and air, you are made of matter. All living and nonliving things are made of matter. Matter is anything that has mass and takes up space. Scientists use different ways to identify matter. One way is by its properties. You can identify many properties of matter by using your senses. For example, you can look at the color, size, and shape of some matter. You can touch matter to decide if its texture is rough or smooth, soft or hard. You can recognize some matter by its smell and taste.

Testing Matter

Simple tests can show other properties of matter. You can see how matter reacts if you heat or cool it, for example. You can see if matter is affected by a magnet or if it allows electricity to pass through it. You can hit matter with a hammer to see if it shatters or is not even dented. You can see how flexible it is. Does it break or does it simply bend however you move it? You can observe what happens when you place matter into water. Does it float or does it sink to the bottom? You can try to mix it with other matter. Does some matter disappear? Or does something new seem to take its place?

1. **✓Checkpoint** Group five different objects in your classroom by properties. Describe the properties.
2. **Art in Science** Collect pictures or small objects that show different textures of matter. Make a collage with the pictures or objects you collect.

319

States of Matter

Using different instruments, scientists have learned that all matter is made up of tiny particles. These particles are arranged in different ways. These particles also move. The arrangement and movement of the particles in matter determine its form, or state. The three most familiar states of matter are solid, liquid, and gas.

Usually substances on Earth exist naturally in just one state. Can you name a substance that you can find naturally in all three states? If you said water, you are right. You can find water naturally in all three forms. Liquid water is the same substance as the solid called ice and the gas called water vapor.

You can't see the particles in a solid. This drawing shows how the tightly packed particles are arranged.

You can't see the particles in a liquid either. The particles are close to each other, but they are not held tightly together.

The particles in a gas are far apart. Even if you could see them, you would not see the particles arranged in any special way.

Solids

At temperatures of 0°C or below, the shape of an ice cube is the same whether it is on a plate or in a container. A solid is matter that has a definite shape and usually takes up a definite amount of space. Its particles are closely packed together. The particles have some energy. They move back and forth, but they do not change places with each other.

Liquids

Water takes the shape of any container into which you pour it. If you pour the water in the container onto a table, its shape changes, but the amount of water stays the same. Matter that does not have a definite shape, but takes up a definite amount of space, is a liquid. In a liquid, the particles are not held together as tightly as in a solid. The particles of a liquid are able to slide past one another.

Gases

In the gas state, water is called water vapor. It is invisible. Water vapor and several other gases make up the air that is all around us. Like a liquid, a gas takes the shape of its container. Unlike a liquid, a gas expands to fill whatever space is available. A gas always fills the container it is in. The particles in a gas are very far apart from one another and move in all directions. Particles in a gas move around more easily and quickly than those in a solid.

✓ Lesson Checkpoint

1. Name the solid and gas forms of water.
2. Draw a diagram to show the arrangement and movement of particles for one state of matter.
3. **Compare and Contrast** the movement of particles in solids, liquids, and gases.

321

Lesson 2

How is matter measured?

You can use metric rulers, balances, and graduated cylinders to measure some properties of matter.

Mass

Did you know that your weight on Earth is about six times as much as your weight on the Moon? That's because your weight depends upon the force of gravity. Your weight on another planet might be much greater than your weight on Earth, but your mass is the same. While your weight on the Moon might be less than your weight on Earth, your mass is the same wherever you go.

Scientists use mass because they want a measurement that will not change if the object is moved to a different location. Mass is the measure of the amount of matter in an object. The mass of an object does not change unless matter is added to or removed from it.

Using a Pan Balance

You can use a pan balance to compare a mass that you know with one that you do not know. When the pans are level, the two masses are equal.

Suppose you found the mass of the toy in the picture and then took it apart. Next you measured the mass of each part separately and added them together. What do think the total would be? The total mass of all the parts is the same as the mass of the assembled toy. The toy's mass is 23 grams.

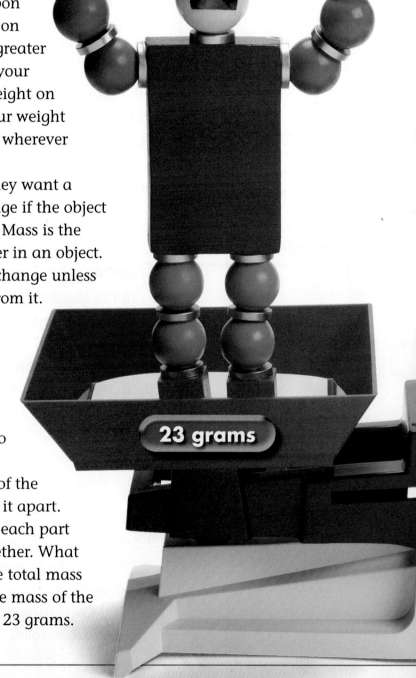

The pan balance shows that the mass of the toy, 23 grams, is equal to the total mass of its parts.

23 grams

Suppose someone who did not see the toy takes all of the parts and makes a toy that looks very different from the one you see. What do you think is the mass of this new toy? That's right, 23 grams. The only way to change the toy's mass is to add parts or not use all of them. This is because the only way to change the total mass of an object is to either add matter or take it away.

Metric Units of Mass

Scientists use metric units when they measure and compare matter. The gram is the base unit of mass in the metric system. Some of the metric units that are used to measure mass are milligram (mg), gram (g), and kilogram (kg).

Like our place-value system, the metric system is based on tens. Prefixes change the base unit to larger or smaller units. For example, 1,000 milligrams are equal to 1 gram, and 1,000 grams are equal to 1 kilogram.

The mass of a large paper clip is about 1 g.

The mass of a nickel is about 5 g.

The mass of the milk in this carton is about 1,000 g, or 1 kg.

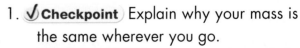

23 grams

1. ✓ **Checkpoint** Explain why your mass is the same wherever you go.
2. **Math in Science** The mass of a nickel is about 5 g. About how many nickels are needed for a mass of 1 kg? Remember that 1 kg = 1,000 g.

323

Volume

Take a deep breath. As your lungs fill with air, you can feel your chest expand. This change in your lung size is an increase in volume. Volume is the amount of space that matter takes up.

Like mass, volume is a property of matter that can be measured. One way to measure the volume of a solid such as a box, is to count the number of unit cubes that fill it. Another way to find the volume is to use a ruler to measure the length, width, and height of the box. Then multiply the measurements. If a box measures 5 cm long, 2 cm wide, and 8 cm high, then the volume of the box is 5 cm $\times$ 2 cm $\times$ 8 cm, or 80 cubic centimeters.

Scientists often use metric units when they measure. The table below shows how the units of length in the metric system are related. Some metric units that are often used to measure and compare the volume of a solid are cubic centimeters (cm^3) and cubic meters (m^3).

The rulers show the box's measurements, which can be multiplied together to find its volume.

Comparing Metric Units of Length

Metric Unit	Equivalent
1 millimeter	0.001 meter
1 centimeter	10 millimeters
1 decimeter	10 centimeters
1 meter	100 centimeters or 1,000 millimeters
1 decameter	10 meters
1 hectometer	100 meters
1 kilometer	1,000 meters

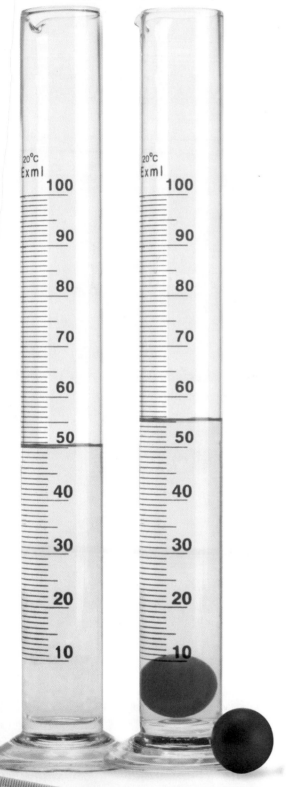

The water level in this graduated cylinder rose from 50 mL to 55 mL when the ball was added. The volume of the ball is 55 mL − 50 mL = 5 mL or 5 cm³.

Volume of Liquids

Liquids do not have a definite shape. To measure a liquid, you use a measuring container, such as a graduated cylinder.

A graduated cylinder is marked with metric units. Some metric units used to measure volume are milliliter (mL) and liter (L). One liter is equal to 1,000 milliliters. The units marked on this graduated cylinder are milliliters (mL).

Volume of Other Objects

A graduated cylinder can be used to find the volume of solids that sink in water. To measure the volume of a ball, for example, put some water into a graduated cylinder. Record its height. Then place the ball into the cylinder, and record the height of the water again. The ball has pushed away some of the water. The water level has risen the same number of milliliters as the volume of the ball. A volume of 1 mL is the same as 1 cm³.

Examples of Metric Lengths

What Was Measured	Measurement
Thickness of a CD	1 mm
Length of a paper clip	32 mm
Thickness of a CD case	1 cm or 10 mm
Height of a doorknob from the floor	1 m
Length of a school bus	12 m
Length of 440 blue whales placed end to end	11 km or 11,000 m
Distance from the North Pole to the equator	10,000 km

1. ✓Checkpoint What metric units are used to measure the volume of solids? of liquids?
2. Math in Science Express 2 L in milliliters.

Density

Sometimes you need to know how much mass is in a certain volume of matter. Suppose a friend asked you, "Which has more mass, a piece of wood or a piece of steel?" Your first response might be, "How big is each piece?" In order to compare the masses of two objects, you need to use an equal volume of each. The amount of mass in a certain volume of matter is a property called **density.** For example, if the pieces of wood and steel are the same size, the piece of steel has more mass and a greater density than the wood.

Finding Density

You find the density of a substance by dividing its mass by its volume. The units often used for the density of solids are grams per cubic centimeter. You write density as a fraction: $\frac{\text{mass in grams}}{\text{volume in cubic centimeters}}$. The density of water is 1 because 1 gram of water has a volume of 1 cubic centimeter.

An object's density determines whether it floats or sinks in a liquid. You can see in the picture at the right that liquids can float on top of other liquids. For example, water floats on top of corn syrup because its density is less than the density of the corn syrup.

cooking oil

water

corn syrup

A peeled orange sinks, but an unpeeled orange floats.

The liquids and other objects have different densities.

Comparing Densities

The substances with the greatest densities are near the bottom of the cylinder. The substances with the least densities are near the top.

You can also compare the densities of the objects that are floating. The density of the grape is less than the density of the corn syrup but greater than the density of water. The density of the plastic block is greater than that of the cooking oil but less than the density of water. The cork has the least density of the liquids and the other objects in the picture.

An ice cube floats in water because the density of ice is less than the density of water. But it's just a little less! So most of a floating ice cube is below the surface.

✓ Lesson Checkpoint

1. Explain why steel sinks in water and cork floats.
2. An unpeeled orange floats in water, but a peeled orange sinks. What can you conclude about the density of an unpeeled orange?
3. **Technology** in Science Scientists use submersibles (submarines) to explore oceans. Use library books or the Internet to find out more about how submarines sink or float.

Life Jacket

Life jackets or life preservers are much smaller than you are. But they help you stay afloat in water. They are filled with foam or other materials that have densities less than water. A life jacket pushes some of the water out of the way just like the ball in the graduated cylinder. The life jacket helps you keep your head above the surface of the water.

Lesson 3

How do substances mix?

Mixtures are made by physically combining two or more substances. The solids, liquids, or gases in a mixture are not chemically combined. They can be easily separated.

Mixtures

You may have eaten a snack made from a mixture of nuts, dried apricots, and raisins. Each ingredient in this mixture keeps its own taste and shape.

A **mixture** is a combination of two or more substances. Substances in a mixture can be separated. This means that they are not chemically combined. Peas, carrots, and corn can be combined in a mixture. In fact, you can buy a bag of frozen mixed vegetables at the store. Each vegetable can be sorted into separate piles. The peas, carrots, and corn taste the same whether they are separated or mixed together. All substances in a mixture that are separated out have the same properties as before they were mixed.

The yellow beads float in water.

A magnet can be used to separate the safety pins from the mixture.

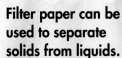

Filter paper can be used to separate solids from liquids.

After the water from the mixture of salt and water evaporated, salt was left behind.

A mixture does not necessarily contain a specific amount of any substance. And the makeup of a mixture can vary. Since parts of a mixture are not joined together chemically, each substance keeps its own properties. You can see the properties of each substance that makes up the mixture shown here. You can use the properties to separate the parts again.

Separating Using Properties

Safety pins are attracted to a magnet. You can use a magnet to separate them from the rest of the mixture shown. You can stir the rest of the mixture into water. Since the beads float, they can be removed. If you pour the mixture into a filter, the sand and the marbles will be trapped. Then, after the water evaporates, the salt will be left.

You separated the parts of this mixture, but you did not change the properties of any of the individual substances.

1. ✓ **Checkpoint** When the bead, marble, sand, and salt mixture is put into water, the yellow beads float. What does this tell you about the density of these yellow beads?

2. **Writing** in Science) **Expository** In your **science journal,** write a numbered set of instructions for separating a mixture of paper clips, wood chips, gravel, and sugar.

Solutions

If you stir salt and water together, you make a mixture. You cannot see the salt in this mixture because it has broken into very small particles. It has dissolved in the water. The salt and water is a special kind of mixture called a solution.

In a **solution,** one or more substances are dissolved in another substance. The most common kind of solution is a solid dissolved in a liquid, such as salt in water. In this kind of solution, the substance that is dissolved is the **solute.** In a solution of salt and water, the salt is the solute. A **solvent** is the substance that takes in, or dissolves, the other substance. Usually there is more solvent than solute. In salt water, the solvent is water.

Common Solutions

In the oceans, salt and other minerals are dissolved in water. Ocean water is a solution. But a solution does not have to be a liquid. The air you breathe, for example, is a solution made up of gases. The steel used for buildings and cars is a solution. During the process of making steel, carbon and iron, two solids, are melted into liquid form. Then the carbon is dissolved in the iron.

The salt is dissolved in this solution.

Salt dissolves in water.

salt

Club soda is a solution made up of a gas dissolved in a liquid. The solubility of the gas decreases as the temperature of the solvent increases. That is why a club soda "goes flat" faster when it gets warm. As the water becomes warmer, more gas leaves the solution.

Instant cocoa dissolves more quickly in a cup of hot water than in a cup of cold water.

Sand does not dissolve in water.

sand

Solubility

No matter what you do, you cannot make sand dissolve in water. The ability of one substance to dissolve in another is called its **solubility.** Solubility is a measure of the amount of a substance that will dissolve in another substance. Since sand does not dissolve in water, the solubility of sand in water is zero.

Sometimes you can speed up the process of dissolving the solute by raising the temperature of the solvent. This is true for most solutes that are solids. For example, you can dissolve more sugar in warm water than you can in cold water.

Another way to make a solute dissolve more quickly is to crush it. If you drop a sugar cube into a cup of water it will dissolve, but it may take a while. If you crush the sugar cube into tiny crystals, the crystals will dissolve very quickly. The reason for this is that more of the sugar particles are touching the water when the sugar is in tiny crystals than when it is in a sugar cube.

✔ Lesson Checkpoint

1. What are the parts of a solution?
2. What factors affect the solubility of a substance?
3. Social Studies in Science During the Gold Rush, many people panned for gold. Panning separates gold from a mixture of gold and other particles such as sand. Use books or the Internet to find out about the California Gold Rush.

A knitter uses a
ball of yarn.

Lesson 4

How does matter change?

Matter undergoes physical and chemical changes. In a physical change, the size, shape, or state of the substance changes. A change that forms a new substance with new properties is a chemical change.

Physical Changes

If you cut and fold a piece of paper to make an origami sculpture, you change only the size and shape of the paper. You have not changed the particles that make up the paper.

A change in the size, shape, or state of matter is a **physical change**. A physical change does not change the particles that make up matter. The arrangement of the particles, however, may be changed.

The yarn is
knitted into a
long strip.

Examples of Physical Changes

Are you causing a physical change when you mix salt and water? A solution of salt and water can be compared to a mixture of nuts and raisins. You can separate the nuts and raisins by hand. In a mixture of salt and water, the particles are too small to be separated by hand. However, if the water evaporates, the salt will be left behind. Because the parts of a mixture do not change and can be separated, making a mixture is an example of a physical change.

Breaking a pencil is a physical change. The pieces of the pencil are still made of wood and graphite. If you sharpen the broken ends, you can keep using the pencil. Another physical change is tearing. If you tear a sheet of paper into tiny pieces, it still is made of the same kind of matter.

The knitted strip
can unravel into
the same amount
of yarn as the
original ball.

Have you ever made a bowl out of clay? You start with a big blob of clay and form it into the shape of a bowl. The clay bowl is made of the same kind of matter as the original blob of clay. The clay is just a different shape. It has changed physically.

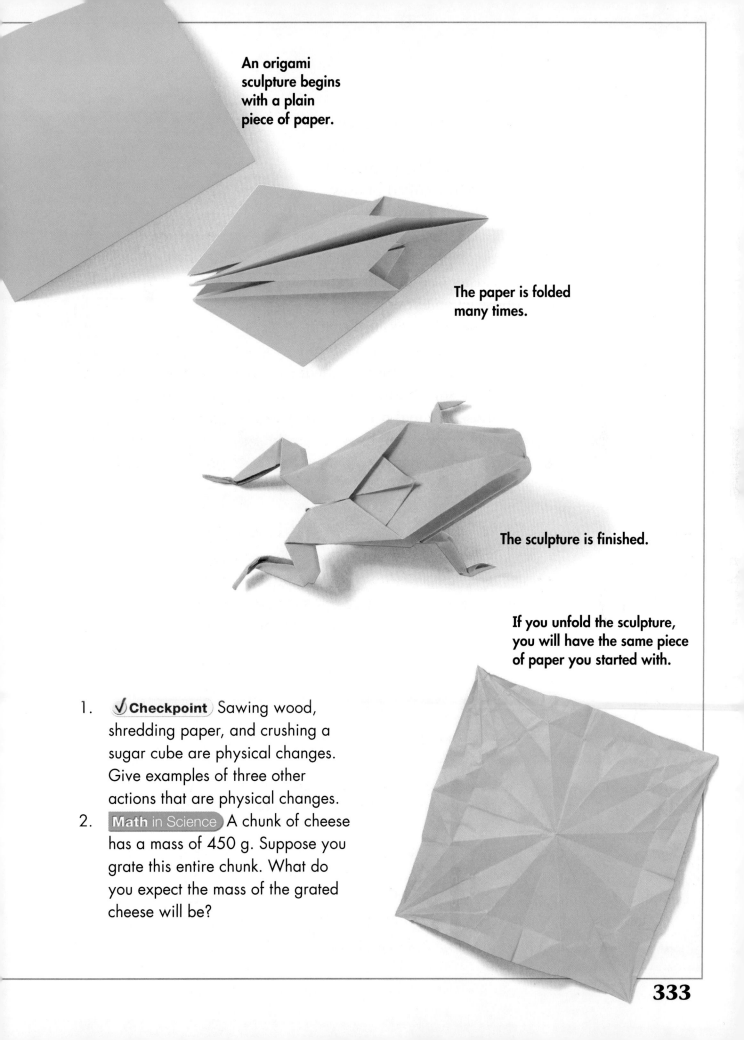

An origami sculpture begins with a plain piece of paper.

The paper is folded many times.

The sculpture is finished.

If you unfold the sculpture, you will have the same piece of paper you started with.

1. ✓ **Checkpoint** Sawing wood, shredding paper, and crushing a sugar cube are physical changes. Give examples of three other actions that are physical changes.

2. **Math** in Science A chunk of cheese has a mass of 450 g. Suppose you grate this entire chunk. What do you expect the mass of the grated cheese will be?

333

Phase Changes

Suppose you freeze water into an ice cube and then let it melt. The liquid that results is still water. Ice and liquid water are the same substance in different states. These states are called phases.

What causes the particles of a substance to be in one phase rather than another? The answer has to do with energy. Energy can cause the particles in a substance to move faster and farther apart. Substances change phase when enough heat energy is added or taken away. For example, you put liquid water into a freezer to remove heat and make ice. You add energy to water when you heat it. If you boil water in a pot, some of the water becomes water vapor. Phase changes are examples of physical changes that can be reversed by adding or removing energy. Every substance changes phases at a different temperature.

Effects of Temperature on Matter

660°C
Aluminum melts.

328°C
Lead melts.

232°C
Tin melts.

100°C
Water boils.
Water vapor condenses.

0°C
Water freezes into ice. Ice melts into water.

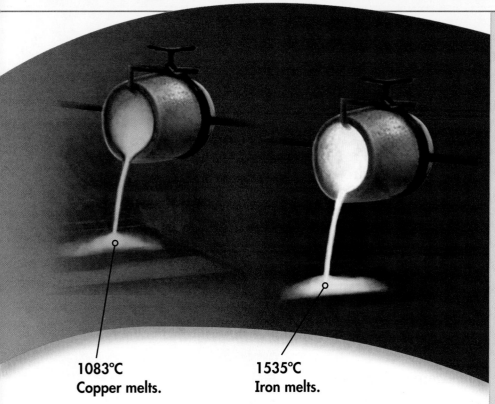

1083°C
Copper melts.

1535°C
Iron melts.

Melting and Boiling Points

The melting point and boiling point of a substance are physical properties that help identify the substance. The melting point is the temperature at which a substance changes from a solid to a liquid. Temperature at which a substance melts is the same temperature at which it freezes, or changes from a liquid to a solid.

The boiling point is the temperature at which a substance changes from a liquid to a gas. This temperature is also the temperature at which the substance changes from a gas back into a liquid.

1. **✓Checkpoint** How does adding or taking away heat energy cause changes in matter?

2. **Writing in Science** **Descriptive** Suppose you are a drop of water. Describe in your **science journal** what happens to you when heat energy is added or taken away.

Energy and Water

These phase changes are examples of physical changes. Whether water is a solid, liquid, or gas, it is still water.

In a solid, the particles are attracted to each other. They are close together and do not move very much.

Adding heat increases the energy of the particles. The particles move faster. Solid ice changes phase by melting into a liquid.

Boiling water adds even more heat energy. The particles move even faster and farther apart. Liquid water changes phase to water vapor.

335

Chemical Changes

If you leave an iron nail in a damp place, it will rust. Suppose you compare the rust with the iron nail. You will find that the nail and the rust have different properties. The color and hardness of rust and iron are different. Rust is a different substance that results from a chemical change in the iron nail. Unlike a physical change, a **chemical change** produces a completely different kind of matter. In a chemical change, particles of one substance are changed in some way to form particles of a new substance with different properties.

You can see evidence of a chemical change, such as the bubbles in the picture. Or the new substance may be a different color. It may have a different smell or temperature. Many chemical changes give off heat. In each case, the chemical properties of the materials that were mixed have changed.

The acid in vinegar reacts with baking soda and forms bubbles of carbon dioxide. The bubbling and fizzing show that a chemical change is occurring.

Rust forms slowly as oxygen from the air combines with the iron in the gear.

Tarnish, like rust, results from a chemical change when certain metals, such as silver, react with air.

Burning wood reacts very quickly with oxygen in the air. The new substances formed by this change are ashes, carbon dioxide gas, and water vapor.

Elements

In a pure substance, particles are alike. The simplest pure substances are called elements. There are more than 100 known elements. Scientists have organized information about these elements in a chart called the Periodic Table. Each element is in a particular row and column in the table. The position in the Periodic Table gives information about the makeup and properties of each element. Each element has its own symbol. The letter or letters in the symbol are sometimes from the element's name in Latin.

The Periodic Table

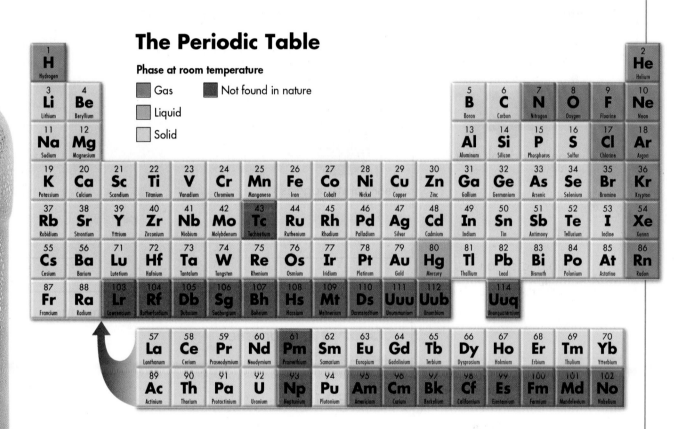

Phase at room temperature
- Gas
- Liquid
- Solid
- Not found in nature

✓ Lesson Checkpoint

1. What is a chemical change?
2. When you chew food, are you causing physical or chemical changes to the food?
3. **Compare and Contrast** How are rusting and burning different? How are they alike?

Lab zone Guided Inquiry

Investigate How can you change the properties of glue?

Mixing glue with another substance can change its properties. The properties of the new substance are different from the properties of the original substances.

Materials

safety goggles

small measuring cup

glue and food coloring

cup and spoon

water   borax solution

Process Skills

After you make **observations,** you can **collect** your **data** in a chart.

What to Do

1 Measure 30 mL of glue into a small measuring cup. Pour it into a larger cup. For fun, add food coloring.

Be careful!

Wear safety goggles.

2 Add 15 mL of water to the cup. Stir the mixture. **Observe** its properties.

3 Add 15 mL of borax solution. Stir.

4 Observe what happens.

338 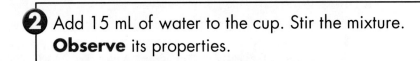 **More** Lab zone **Activities** Take It to the Net
pearsonsuccessnet.com

Could you do this with glue?

5 Play with the new mixture. **Investigate** its properties.

Wash your hands when finished.

6 Record the **data** you **collect** about the properties of the glue and of the new substance.

Property	Observations	
	Glue	New Substance
Color		
Texture		
State of Matter (solid, liquid, gas)		
Odor		

Explain Your Results

1. Based on the **data** you **collected,** tell how are the physical properties of the new substance and the glue alike. What differences did you **observe**?

2. Would the new substance be a good glue? Explain.

Go Further

If you used a different amount of borax solution, would the substance have the same properties? Develop a plan for a safe, simple investigation to answer this question or one of your own. With teacher permission, carry out the plan you designed.

Comparing Densities

The table lists some common liquids and their densities. Each density is rounded to the nearest tenth.

	Substance	Density ($\frac{\text{grams}}{\text{cubic centimeters}}$)
A	Corn Syrup	1.4
B	Cooking Oil	0.9
C	Ethyl Alcohol	0.8
D	Gasoline	0.7
E	Water	1.0

Density is written as a decimal number. You can use a number line to compare and order decimals. On a number line, the values increase as you move to the right and decrease as you move to the left. For example, on the number line below, 0.7 is less than 0.9, so 0.7 is to the left of 0.9.

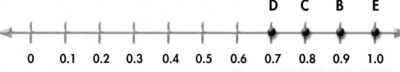

Use the table and number line on page 340 to answer the following questions.

❶ Which point on the number line represents the density of cooking oil?
  A. Point E   B. Point B
  C. Point C   D. Point D

❷ Where on the number line would you plot the point for the density of corn syrup?
  F. to the left of Point D
  G. to the left of Point E
  H. at Point E
  I. to the right of Point E

❸ How many liquids in the table have a greater density than gasoline has?
  A. 1   B. 2
  C. 3   D. 4

❹ Suppose you poured liquids A–E into a graduated cylinder. Which is the correct order of liquid layers from **bottom** to **top**?
  F. D, B, C, E, A
  G. D, C, B, A, E
  H. A, D, C, B, E
  I. A, E, B, C, D

Lab zone Take-Home Activity

An object with a density that is less than $1.0 \frac{gram}{cubic\ centimeter}$ floats in water. List ten items from your home. Predict whether each item will float or sink. Record your predictions. Then test each item. Indicate which items have a density that is less than $1.0 \frac{gram}{cubic\ centimeter}$.

Chapter 11 Review and Test Prep

Use Vocabulary

chemical change (p. 336)	**solubility** (p. 331)
density (p. 326)	**solute** (p. 330)
mixture (p. 328)	**solution** (p. 330)
physical change (p. 332)	**solvent** (p. 330)

Use the vocabulary term from the list above that completes each sentence.

1. _____ is the ability of one substance to dissolve in another substance.

2. The property that compares the mass of an object with its volume is _____.

3. In a solution, the _____ is the substance that takes in, or dissolves, the other substance.

4. A change in size, shape, or state of matter is a _____.

5. The substance in a solution that is dissolved is called the _____.

6. The quarters, dimes, nickels, and pennies in a coin purse are a _____.

7. New substances with different properties are formed by a _____.

8. In a _____, substances are dissolved in other substances.

Explain Concepts

9. What does it mean to say that a liquid has a definite volume but no definite shape?

10. Suppose you have 50 mL of water in a graduated cylinder. After you place a marble in the cylinder, the water level rises to 78 mL. What is the volume of the marble? Explain how you know.

Process Skills

11. **Infer** A balloon filled with helium gas rises in the air. What might you infer about the density of helium compared with the density of air?

12. **Classify** Tell whether each of the following involves a physical change or a chemical change.
- frying an egg
- breaking a balloon
- boiling water
- toasting bread

13. Observe Suppose you put a substance in a glass of water and stir the mixture. Then you observe that all of the substance settles to the bottom of the glass. From your observation, what might you conclude about the solubility of the substance?

Compare and Contrast

14. Explain how physical and chemical changes are different. How are they alike? Use a graphic organizer like the one shown.

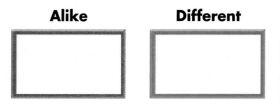

Alike	**Different**

Test Prep

Choose the letter that best completes the statement or answers the question.

15. Matter is anything that has mass and
ⓐ is living.
ⓑ takes up space.
ⓒ is not broken.
ⓓ holds water or air.

16. When most liquids are cooled to the freezing point, the tiny particles of matter that make up the liquid
Ⓕ move quickly in all directions.
Ⓖ move out into the air.
Ⓗ come closer together.
Ⓘ move farther apart.

17. A chemical change results in a
ⓐ loss of matter or energy.
ⓑ solution.
ⓒ phase change.
ⓓ different kind of matter.

18. You make a solution when you mix
Ⓕ salt and water.
Ⓖ sugar and cinnamon.
Ⓗ vegetables in a salad.
Ⓘ cheese sauce and macaroni.

19. Explain why the answer you chose for Question 16 is best. For each of the answers you did not choose, give a reason why it is not the best choice.

20. ⟨Writing in Science⟩ **Expository** Since ice is less dense than liquid water, it floats. Explain what you think would happen to the plants and animals living in a Minnesota pond if ice were more dense than liquid water.

Analytical Chemist

Dionne Broxton Jackson is an analytical chemist at NASA. She works with metals.

What if your pencil bent every time you tried to write with it? What if your pillow were made of metal? All of the properties of matter are important in deciding how it is used. Matter can be hard or soft, rough or smooth. It can be sticky, stretchy, spongy, or slick. Some chemists who work for NASA make matter that can be used on space vehicles.

Metals used for space shuttles must not be damaged by a lot of heat. Some metals are better than others at handling heat. Chemists can also mix metals to make a material that can stand more heat than either metal could on its own. The Kennedy Space Center is close to the ocean. There is so much salty water nearby that metals often rust. The metals NASA uses cannot rust easily.

Plastics are also important materials used in space. They may need to be hard and slick, or soft and rubbery. Chemists can make plastics that have many different properties.

Analytical chemists need to understand math and science well. They must graduate from a college or university. They can work in many different places.

Lab zone Take-Home Activity

Gather different materials in your home, such as kitchen utensils, toothbrushes, and food containers. Make a list in your **science journal** of which products you think might be useful in space.

EC CRU 10 9 8 7 6 5 4 3 2 1

You Will Discover

○ the difference between heat and temperature.
○ three ways heat is transferred.

Chapter 12
Heat

online
Student Edition
pearsonsuccessnet.com

How does heat energy move from one object to another?

thermal energy

conductor

insulator

346

Chapter 12 Vocabulary

conduction

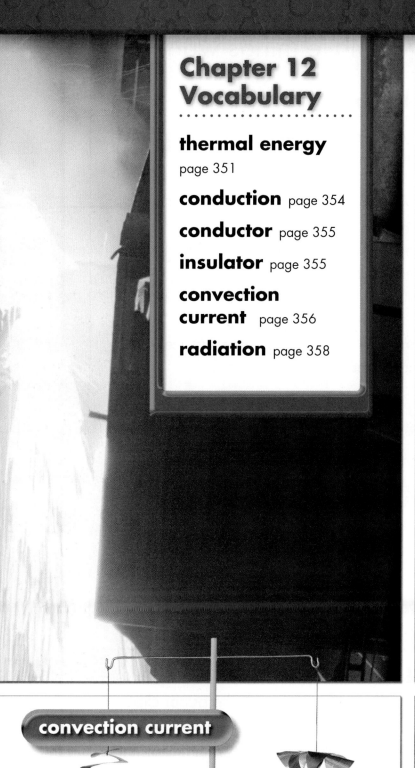

convection current

radiation

347

Explore How can you make things warmer?

Materials

safety goggles

paper clip

eraser

sheet of paper

clock with a second hand
(or timer or stopwatch)

What to Do

1 Touch a paper clip. **Observe**.
Does it feel warm?

Be careful!

The paper clip
could break.

2 Bend one end back and forth
4 times quickly. Quickly touch
the bent part. Observe.

3 Touch an eraser. Rub it on paper
for 1 minute. Quickly touch the surface you
rubbed on the paper. Observe.

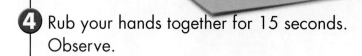

4 Rub your hands together for 15 seconds.
Observe.

Process Skills

You can use what
you learn by
observation
to help you
make accurate
inferences.

Explain Your Results

1. How did bending change the paper clip?
2. What did you **observe** when you rubbed
   the eraser against paper? What happened
   when you rubbed one hand against the other?
3. What can you **infer** about what happens
   when one object rubs against another?

How to Read Science

Reading Skills

Cause and Effect

A **cause** may have more than one **effect.** An effect may have more than one cause. An effect may cause something else to happen. Clues such as *because, so, since, thus,* and *as a result* that signal cause and effect can also help you **make inferences.**

Think about what you know and have observed about hot-air balloons and heat transfer as you read the interview with a balloonist. Cause and effect are highlighted.

Magazine Interview

Extreme Sports
for Kids!

Extreme Sports for Kids: I understand that you enjoy riding in hot-air balloons. Just what causes a hot-air balloon to rise?

Balloonist: It all results from heat transfer. A balloon is like a huge plastic bag. To inflate the bag, I fill it with air. Then I heat that air with a burner. A flame reaches into the plastic bag.

ESK: Then does heat transfer take place?

Balloonist: Yes, the air inside the bag gets warm and less dense than the air around it. The cool air sinks under the warmer air. As a result, the balloon goes up!

ESK: I know that air expands when it gets heated because particles are moving really fast and really far apart!

Balloonist: You're right. Let's take a ride!

Apply It!
Make a graphic organizer to help you **infer** why a hot-air balloon rises.

Cause		Effect

You Are There!

The red-hot steel flows into an iron mold. Even though you are wearing a suit that protects you from the heat, you can sense the scorching air! You work in one of the world's most important industries. You are a steelworker. At your mill, iron ores from rocks and minerals are crushed and then heated in giant furnaces. They become liquid steel. Your job is to cast that molten steel into 2-ton blocks called ingots. The steel that you pour hardens into an ingot. The ingot is placed in a huge heated pit where the temperature reaches 1200°C (2,200°F). How does heat move?

AudioText

Why does matter have energy?

Energy is the ability to cause change or do work. Heat is the total energy of moving particles in matter. The more particles something has, the more internal energy it contains.

Energy in Matter

Rub your hands together. What happens? You just used energy to make heat! Energy is the ability to change something or do work. Cool hands changed to warm ones. Whenever the location, makeup, or look of something changes, energy is used. All changes need energy!

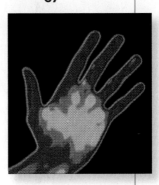

The colors in this thermogram, or heat picture, show the different amounts of heat energy.

All matter is made up of tiny particles that are always moving. In a solid, particles are closely packed. They move slightly around fixed positions. In a liquid, they are close together. They flow freely past one another. In a gas, particles are very far apart. They move in all directions. Particles in an object move because they have energy.

As an object becomes hotter, its particles move faster. As the object cools, the particles move more slowly. **Thermal energy** is energy due to moving particles that make up matter. We feel the flow of thermal energy as heat.

1. ✔**Checkpoint** What is energy?
2. **Writing in Science** **Descriptive** You are in a sunny place wearing a T-shirt and shorts. Write a paragraph in your **science journal** that describes changes to you and to a piece of chocolate on a table near you.

a bulb that holds colored alcohol. The number lines marked on the outside of the tube show degrees. One number line is scaled in degrees Celsius. The other is scaled in degrees Fahrenheit. A thermometer is based on the idea that matter expands when its particles move faster and contracts when they slow down.

If a thermometer touches matter with particles that are speeding up, particles in the liquid inside the thermometer speed up too. They move farther apart. Because the liquid expands more than the glass tube, it moves up the tube. The reading on the number line shows a greater number of degrees. If the particles slow down, the liquid contracts. The shorter column in the tube shows fewer degrees.

The thermometer must be on or in whatever it's measuring. If it's not touching the material, it might not measure particle motion correctly.

How a Thermometer Works

This thin glass tube has a bulb filled with colored alcohol. The bulb is placed on or in the material being measured. Depending on the material's temperature, liquid travels up or down the tube. The thermometer in the photo is measuring the temperature of the air. The number lines on the outside of the tube show degrees Celsius on the right and degrees Fahrenheit on the left.

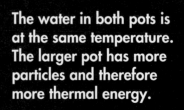

The water in both pots is at the same temperature. The larger pot has more particles and therefore more thermal energy.

Heat and Temperature

If you wonder how hot or cold something is, you might think about its temperature. When a material has a high temperature, its particles move fast. But temperature is not a measure of how much heat the material has.

Many of us mix up the meanings of heat and temperature. The difference is in the movement of particles of matter. Temperature is the measure of the average amount of motion of particles in matter. It measures the average energy. Thermal energy is the total energy of those moving particles. It measures both how fast the particles move and how many are moving. Heat is the transfer of thermal energy from one piece of matter to another.

For example, think of a large pot and a small pot that are each half filled with boiling water. Because the large pot holds more water, it has many more water particles than the small pot has. More particles mean more energy of motion. The large pot has more thermal energy. Since the water in each pot is boiling, the temperature of the water in both pots is the same. The average amount of motion of particles in the water is also the same. So, the size of the pot does not affect temperature!

Fewer particles in the smaller pot mean less thermal energy.

100°C

✓ Lesson Checkpoint

1. What happens to the motion of particles when an object becomes hotter?
2. Explain why a large pot of water takes longer to begin boiling than a small pot. Both pots started with the same temperature of water, and burners for both pots are set on "high."
3. 🔄 Cause and Effect What causes liquid in a thermometer to travel up and down the tube?

Lesson 2

How does heat move?

Heat is the transfer of thermal energy. Heat can be moved in several ways. The transfer of heat energy affects climate.

Conduction

Thermal energy flows from something warm to something cool. The transfer of thermal energy between matter with different temperatures is heat. A heat source is anything that gives off energy that particles of matter can take in.

Remember when you rubbed your hands together earlier? You used mechanical energy to make heat. When solids are touching, heat energy moves by conduction. **Conduction** is the transfer of heat energy by one thing touching another.

Heat energy from the water moves through the metal spoon. The heat causes the piece of wax to melt.

A Conduction Experiment

Suppose that you stick wax on the handle of a metal spoon. Then you place the lower part of the spoon in boiling water. The spoon's particles that touch the water start to move. As they move more quickly, they crash into other particles in the spoon. Soon, heat energy from the water moves throughout the spoon. Heat transfer continues until the water and the spoon are the same temperature. How do we know that the heat energy has moved? The hot spoon handle and the melting wax are proof! A wooden spoon does not conduct heat energy well. Its handle stays cooler. A piece of wax on the wooden spoon doesn't melt.

Conductors and Insulators

Metal Some materials let heat move through them more easily than others do. A material that readily allows heat to move is a **conductor**—like the metal spoon. Many metals, such as aluminum, copper, and iron, conduct heat well. If you place an iron pan on a burner or other heat source, it gets hot quickly.

Wood You also know that some things—like the wooden spoon—do not get too warm even when they touch something hot. They are insulators. An **insulator** is a material that limits the amount of heat that passes through it. Have you noticed that many pots and pans have wooden handles? That's because wood is a great insulator. The wooden paddle in the photo does not conduct heat to the hands of the person taking the pizza from a hot oven. Heat moves around the paddle.

Marble Since ancient times, marble has been used in buildings and monuments because it is strong and beautiful. It resists fires and erosion. Marble is also an insulator. A slab of marble is helpful in the kitchen. Its cool, smooth surface is a perfect place to mix tasty treats.

Plastic Do you know why so many foods are served in foam containers? The plastic foam that is used to make the containers has many small air pockets. The plastic is not the only insulator. Air is a good insulator, too. The plastic and air insulators keep the food at the right temperature.

1. ✓**Checkpoint** What is the difference between an insulator and a conductor?
2. **Social Studies** in Science
    Use reference sources such as encyclopedias, nonfiction books, and the Internet to find other materials that are used as insulators. Explain where the material is used and how it works as an insulator.

The raised hairs of Japanese macaque monkeys trap heat. The monkeys share body heat to keep warm in the snow.

Convection

Have you felt how warm a kitchen gets when a stove is on? The warmth is the result of convection. In convection, a gas or a liquid moves from place to place. A pattern of flowing heat energy is a **convection current.** A convection current forms when gas or liquid transfers heat as it moves.

Heated air is less dense than cooler air around it. The cooler air sinks down. The warm air is forced up. The cool air is warmed by a heat source. This newly-warmed air is forced upward by colder air. The pattern continues.

Look at the two mobiles in the photo below. Can you find the heat source? It's the candles. As each burning candle heats the air above it, the air particles move faster. The particles move farther apart as they take in the energy, making the air less dense. Cooler air rushes under the less dense air. It pushes the warmer air upward. As long as each candle—a heat source—is burning, movement of the rising warm air will make the spiral twirl and the blades spin.

One kind of much larger convection current shapes our weather. Uneven heating of the air around Earth causes currents that cover thousands of kilometers. They make Earth's major wind patterns.

1. ✓ **Checkpoint** How does a convection current form?
2. **Math in Science** Choose a major city in your state. Use the Internet or other sources to find the average temperature for each month of the year. Display your data in a bar graph.

SciLinks **Take It to the Net** keyword: convection current
pearsonsuccessnet.com code: g4p356

Radiators in Buildings

A radiator heats the air by convection. Water is heated in a boiler. Then the hot water or steam is pumped into pipes throughout the building. The pipes lead into radiators in each room. Radiators are made of metal. Some of the heat energy from the the hot water or steam passes through the radiator into the air. Convection currents move the air to heat the entire room. The cooler water returns from the radiator to the boiler through another pipe. The heating cycle begins again.

Warm fluid is less dense.

Cooler fluid is more dense.

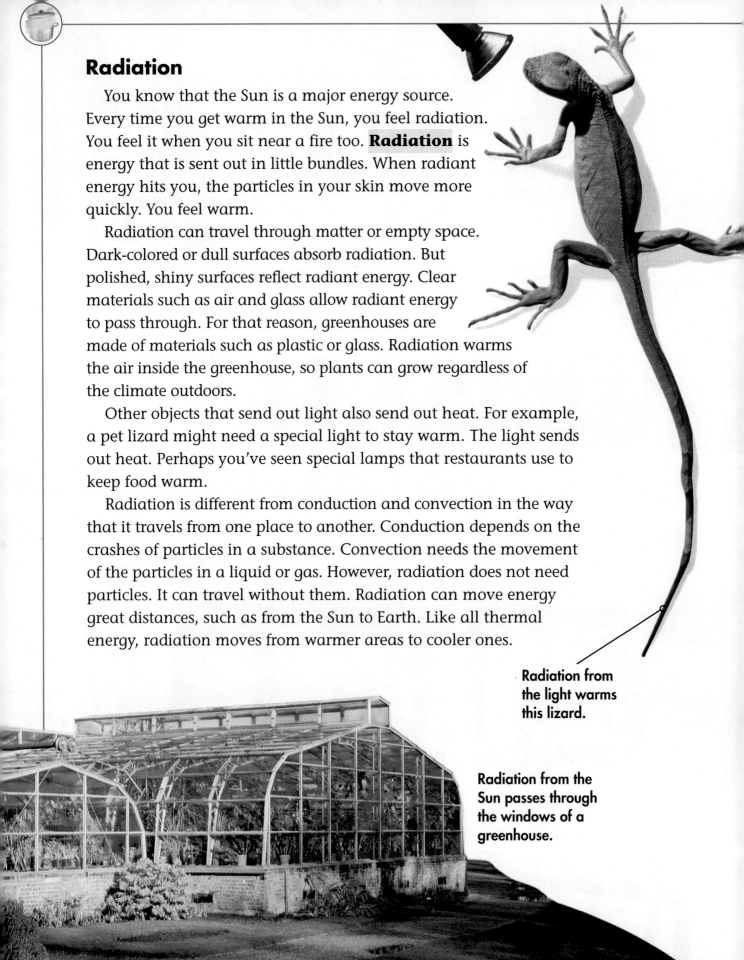

Radiation

You know that the Sun is a major energy source. Every time you get warm in the Sun, you feel radiation. You feel it when you sit near a fire too. **Radiation** is energy that is sent out in little bundles. When radiant energy hits you, the particles in your skin move more quickly. You feel warm.

Radiation can travel through matter or empty space. Dark-colored or dull surfaces absorb radiation. But polished, shiny surfaces reflect radiant energy. Clear materials such as air and glass allow radiant energy to pass through. For that reason, greenhouses are made of materials such as plastic or glass. Radiation warms the air inside the greenhouse, so plants can grow regardless of the climate outdoors.

Other objects that send out light also send out heat. For example, a pet lizard might need a special light to stay warm. The light sends out heat. Perhaps you've seen special lamps that restaurants use to keep food warm.

Radiation is different from conduction and convection in the way that it travels from one place to another. Conduction depends on the crashes of particles in a substance. Convection needs the movement of the particles in a liquid or gas. However, radiation does not need particles. It can travel without them. Radiation can move energy great distances, such as from the Sun to Earth. Like all thermal energy, radiation moves from warmer areas to cooler ones.

Radiation from the light warms this lizard.

Radiation from the Sun passes through the windows of a greenhouse.

358

Conduction, Convection, and Radiation

Once the Sun's energy reaches Earth, Earth's surface heats up. Then conduction takes place. Earth's surface transfers heat to the air. Earth warms the air around you. And Earth is heated by the Sun.

But it's not just conduction that is happening! Convection currents form as the air is heated by Earth's surface. That warm air expands and rises. As the rising air cools, the water vapor in it condenses and falls to Earth as rain or snow. Convection currents in the air cause Earth's wind and rain patterns.

Sun

Radiant energy

Earth

The radiant energy from the Sun warms Earth's surface.

✓ Lesson Checkpoint

1. How does energy from the Sun reach Earth?
2. **⊙ Cause and Effect** What causes Earth's surface to get warm?
3. Writing in Science **Expository** In your **science journal,** write a paragraph that explains why a greenhouse might be part of a flower shop.

Investigate How are thermal energy and temperature different?

Materials

measuring cup and warm water

2 large cups and 2 thermometers

ice cubes

2 plastic spoons

masking tape

What to Do

1 **Measure** carefully. Pour 300 mL of warm water into cup A. Pour 150 mL of warm water into cup B.

Label the cups.

A

B

150 mL

300 mL

2 Record the temperature of the water in each cup.

	Temperature of Water (°C)	
	Cup A (300 mL water)	**Cup B** (150 mL water)
Before adding ice		
After 1 ice cube melts		
After 2 ice cubes melt		
After 3 ice cubes melt		
After 4 ice cubes melt		
After 5 ice cubes melt		
Number of ice cubes completely melted when temperature reached 10°C		

3 Put an ice cube in each cup. Stir each cup gently. Record the water temperature.

4 After a cup's ice cube melts, record the water temperature in that cup. Add another ice cube to that cup.

5 When the temperature in a cup reaches 10°C, stop adding ice cubes to that cup.

Keep stirring until the ice cubes melt!

Make a bar graph to show your data.

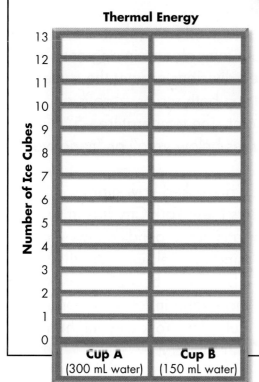

Thermal Energy

To organize and display your data, construct a chart and a graph like the ones shown. They will help you examine, analyze, and evaluate the information.

Interpret your chart and graph and those of other groups. Share your results. Do not change your results just because they are different from those of other groups.

Explain Your Results

1. Which cup had more thermal energy? How do you know?

2. Suppose you used 600 mL of your warm water. **Predict** how many ice cubes would be needed to lower the temperature to 10°C. How could you test your prediction?

Go Further

Develop and conduct a scientific investigation to test the prediction you made. Design any tables, charts, graphs, or diagrams to help record, display, and interpret your data.

Using Temperature Scales

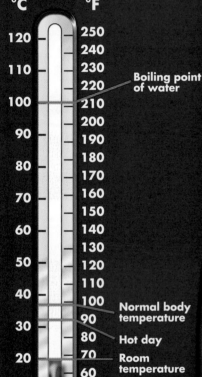

°C   °F

°C	°F	
120	250	
	240	
110	230	Boiling point
	220	of water
100	210	
	200	
90	190	
	180	
80	170	
70	160	
	150	
60	140	
	130	
50	120	
	110	
40	100	Normal body
30	90	temperature
	80	Hot day
20	70	Room
	60	temperature
10	50	Cool day
	40	
0	30	Freezing point of water
	20	
-10	10	Cold day
-20	0	Very cold day
	-10	
-30	-20	
	-30	
-40	-40	
	-50	
-50		

Both the Celsius and Fahrenheit temperature scales measure temperature in degrees (°), but the degree divisions are not the same.

Notice that, on both scales, zero is a label for a point. The temperature −5° is read "5 degrees below zero" or "negative 5 degrees."

Suppose you are asked how many 40-degree days New York City has in January. Your answer depends on the scale being used. Using the Celsius scale, the answer would be "zero" because New York City is never that warm in January—or in any other month! But, New York City might get as warm as 40°F in January.

Decide which temperature scale is being used in each situation: the Fahrenheit scale or the Celsius scale.

1. The outdoor thermometer reads 25 degrees, and you are water skiing.

2. The temperature is 40 degrees and you are wearing a coat at an outdoor football game.

3. The weather report uses "below freezing" and "above zero" to describe the same temperature.

4. You heat water to 100 degrees, but the water does not boil.

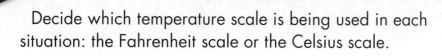

Lab zone Take-Home Activity

Find three different kinds of thermometers at home. They might include a weather thermometer, a fever thermometer, and a meat thermometer. Make a list of the three kinds and record the highest temperature on the Fahrenheit or Celsius scale for each one. Write a paragraph explaining why they are different for different thermometers.

Chapter 12 Review and Test Prep

Use Vocabulary

conduction (p. 354)	insulator (p. 355)
conductor (p. 355)	radiation (p. 358)
convection current (p. 356)	thermal energy (p. 351)

Use the vocabulary term from the list above that completes each sentence.

1. The total energy of all the particles in a body is its _____.

2. A(n) _____ limits the amount of heat that passes through it.

3. _____ is one kind of energy that travels from the Sun through space.

4. A material that allows heat to pass through it is a(n) _____.

5. In a(n) _____, a heated liquid or gas rises and is replaced by cooler liquid or gas.

6. The transfer of energy by one object touching another is _____.

Explain Concepts

7. Explain how particles move differently in a solid, a liquid, and a gas.

8. Explain why the motion of particles affects a thermometer reading.

Process Skills

9. **Infer** why young trees and plants are sometimes kept in greenhouses before they are planted outdoors.

10. **Make a model** that shows how heat moves through objects.

11. **Predict** On a bright, sunny day, you are sitting next to the ice rink of an outdoor hockey game. Which will keep you warmer: a dark, wool blanket or a clear, plastic sheet?

Cause and Effect

12. Fill in the missing cause and effect to show how heat is transferred in each situation.

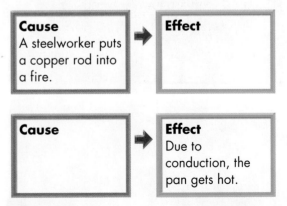

Cause	Effect
A steelworker puts a copper rod into a fire.	

Cause	Effect
	Due to conduction, the pan gets hot.

 Test Prep

Choose the letter that best completes the statement or answers the question.

13. Which is the best conductor?
  Ⓐ metal
  Ⓑ wood
  Ⓒ marble
  Ⓓ plastic

14. Temperature is a measure of
  Ⓕ the total amount of energy in an object's moving particles.
  Ⓖ the average amount of motion of an object's particles.
  Ⓗ the amount of energy transferred from the environment to the particles of an object.
  Ⓘ the size of an object's particles.

15. A large pot of boiling water has more thermal energy than a small pot of boiling water. The temperature of the water is
  Ⓐ higher in the large pot.
  Ⓑ higher in the small pot.
  Ⓒ impossible to measure.
  Ⓓ the same in both pots.

16. A thermometer measures temperature by showing
  Ⓕ particles.
  Ⓖ climate.
  Ⓗ degrees.
  Ⓘ volume.

17. When two solids touch, thermal energy transfers by
  Ⓐ insulation.
  Ⓑ conduction.
  Ⓒ convection currents.
  Ⓓ liquids.

18. The Sun warms your skin by
  Ⓕ insulation.
  Ⓖ radiation.
  Ⓗ conduction.
  Ⓘ convection.

19. Explain why the answer you selected for Question 13 is best. For each of the answers you did not select, give a reason why it is not the best choice.

20. ⬤Writing in Science⬤ **Informative**
Use the Internet to research solar ovens. Find out what foods can be cooked in them and how cooking times compare with those of conventional ovens. Write an informative paragraph to share your findings.

Managing Heat Transfer

Did you know that the research NASA uses to launch people into space helps people on Earth? For example, some NASA scientists are part of the Thermal Protection Materials and Systems Branch. Their task is to develop TPS (Thermal Protection System) materials that protect spacecraft and astronauts from heat. Their research produces materials that are lightweight, yet strong and heat-resistant—materials like those needed to protect steel workers, fire fighters, and others.

Some of the TPS material looks like a carpet. You can roll it out, cut it to shape, and even walk on it! NASA's scientists are testing it to find how well it performs.

NASA uses TPS materials in heat shields that guard spacecraft when they enter other atmospheres or come back to Earth's. One material was used on the Mars *Pathfinder* space probe.

But the research provides information for people on Earth too. NASA's scientists use what they know about heat transfer to help others. In East Africa, many people use wood to cook food. But wood is hard to find. In some parts of Africa, people spend over half the money they earn each year on cooking fuel.

One of NASA's energy management programs uses satellite information to study Earth from a global point of view. NASA's Surface Solar Energy (SSE) information lets people use their latitude and longitude to learn the amount of solar energy available for cooking and many other purposes. Solar Cookers International, a group that helps others learn to cook with the Sun, can zoom in on the places where solar cooking can be best used.

NASA's SSE information helps East Africans use the Sun, a natural resource and great source of heat energy, to cook. Then the people don't need to hunt for wood or spend what little money they have on fuel.

With the Sun's energy, East Africans use solar cookers to prepare meals. The Sun is a safe and clean heat source. Solar cooking does not cost much. It does not cause a lot of smoke or air pollution in the environment. Solar cooking helps people harness some of the Sun's power!

Lab zone Take-Home Activity

Would you rather work as a scientist who studies TPS materials or as one who studies SSE? Tell a partner which job you'd prefer and why.

Max Planck

Max Planck was a German physicist who lived from 1858 to 1947. A physicist is a scientist who studies matter and energy. While studying heat and radiant energy, he noticed the ways that hot surfaces sent out light and took in radiant energy. Planck said that objects were able to send out and take in radiation in only little bunches. Planck called those bunches quanta. His ideas became known as the quantum theory.

Planck's ideas about energy quanta were different from past ideas. Scientists believed energy flowed without stopping. They knew that at times energy acted like a wave, but at other times, it acted like a collection of particles.

Then, another physicist, Albert Einstein, used Planck's theory to explain his own ideas. Einstein said that light is quantized. He meant that things that send out light do so in little bundles of energy. He thought that radiation was made up of particles, not waves.

The work of one scientist plays a part in the work of others. Planck's ideas affected Einstein's! Scientists now know that radiation has qualities of both particles and waves.

Max Planck changed physics with his theory about radiant energy.

Lab zone Take-Home Activity

The little bundles of energy that Planck described are the power source for solar cookers. Use the Internet or other resources to find other devices that use solar energy.

EC.CRU 10 9 8 7 6 5 4 3 2 1

Chapter 13
Electricity and Magnetism

You Will Discover

- what causes objects to become charged.
- how electricity moves.
- why a compass needle points north-south.
- ways that electricity and magnetism are related.
- how magnetism can be transformed into electricity.

Discovery Channel School
Student DVD

online
Student Edition
pearsonsuccessnet.com

What are some ways that energy can be changed from one type to another?

static electricity

series circuit

parallel circuit

370

Chapter 13 Vocabulary

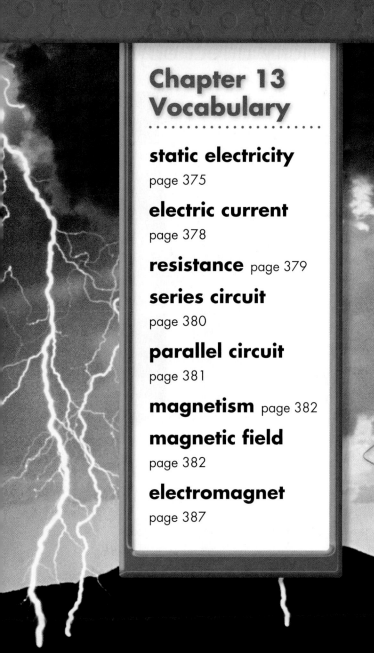

electric current

resistance

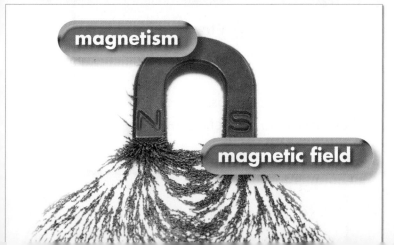

magnetism

magnetic field

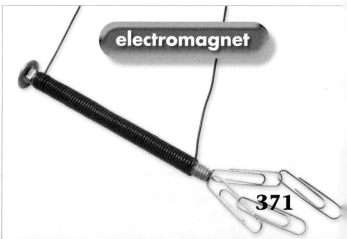

electromagnet

371

Lab zone: Directed Inquiry

Explore How can static electricity affect objects?

Materials

safety goggles

balloon and string

wool cloth

What to Do

1 Tie a string to a balloon. Rub the balloon with a wool cloth for about 1 minute.

Rubbing causes your balloon to have a negative charge and your cloth to have a positive charge.

Rub ALL parts of your balloon!

The balloon has a negative charge.

The cloth has a positive charge.

2 Hold your balloon by the string. Hold your cloth about an arm's length away. Gradually bring them closer together. **Observe**.

3 Rub *ALL* parts of your balloon again. Hold it by the string. Slowly bring it near the balloon of another group. Observe.

The effect you observe is caused by static electricity.

Both balloons have a negative charge.

Explain Your Results

1. What happened as you brought together your balloon and your cloth? your balloon and the balloon of another group?

2. **Infer** How do objects with opposite charges affect each other? How do objects with the same charge affect each other?

Reading Skills

Cause and Effect

Learning to find **causes and effects** can help you understand what you read. A cause may have more than one effect. An effect may have more than one cause. Words such as *because, so,* and *as a result* may signal cause and effect. Sometimes you can **infer** cause and effect based on what you've observed.

Causes and effects are marked in the advertisement below.

Magazine Advertisement

Feeling positively negative about clinging clothes?
Does static electricity rub you the wrong way?
Take charge! Try ELECTRO-NOT!

This new spray tames static electricity. Spray it on socks before putting them in the dryer. They won't stick to your shirts. Your hair will no longer stand up when you remove your winter hat. Using our patented anti-cling technology, ELECTRO-NOT neutralizes the charges that build up on your clothing. Let the sparks fly in your campfire, not on your clothes. Buy ELECTRO-NOT today. Your socks will be glad you did!

Apply It!

Use the **causes and effects** and **inferences** you can make from the advertisement to complete a graphic organizer.

| Cause | → | Effect |

You Are There!

ZZZAPP! A jagged bolt of lightning slashes and flashes through the sky. Less than a second later, it's gone. But then more and more brilliant bolts appear, briefly connecting the clouds to the ground. Like snowflakes and grains of sand, each bolt is unique. BOOOOM!! The sound of thunder startles you. You are glad that you are indoors, watching this dazzling "spark-a-palooza" through a window. What causes this beautiful, super-charged sight that can pack a deadly wallop?

AudioText

Lesson 1

How does matter become charged?

What causes a thundercloud to make lightning? Why do socks cling in the dryer? The answer is static electricity.

Electric Charges

You dash across a carpet and touch a metal doorknob. OUCH! A jolt of static electricity and a small spark startle you.

To understand what happened, start with atoms, the tiny building blocks of everything. A sheet of paper is about one million atoms thick. Almost all atoms have three different particles. Some particles have a positive charge (+), some have a negative charge (–), and some have no charge. Matter usually has the same number of positive particles as negative particles. It is neutral.

Charged particles can move between objects that are close to each other. **Static electricity** happens when positive and negative charges no longer balance. *Static* means "not moving," but eventually the static electricity does move. It may move gradually or it may move very quickly. Moving charges generate electrical energy, which changes into sound, light, and heat energy.

Static Electricity

As charged particles move between atoms in storm clouds, the clouds become charged. Usually, the positive particles cluster near the top and the negative particles gather near the bottom of the clouds. In time, this static electrical energy is released as lightning. It heats up the surrounding air, making it glow. Lightning also creates a mighty sound—thunder.

1. ✓**Checkpoint** What causes static electricity on an object?
2. **Social Studies** in Science Benjamin Franklin invented the lightning rod. Use the Internet or other resources to find out what a lightning rod does.

How Charged Objects Behave

You can predict how charged objects will behave. If two objects have opposite charges—if one is positive and the other is negative—they will pull toward each other. This attraction causes an electric force. An electric force is the pull or push between objects that have a different charge.

A charged object can attract something that has no charge. If you rub a balloon on your hair, it picks up negative particles. It becomes negatively charged. Then, if you hold the balloon near lightweight neutral objects, such as scraps of paper, they move toward it. The balloon will stick to a wall because the negative charge repels the negative charges in the wall. The part of the wall near the balloon is positively charged. After a while, the balloon loses its charge and falls off the wall.

Suppose you are wearing a wool cap on a chilly winter day. While you wear the cap, negative particles move from your hair to the cap. As a result, each strand of hair becomes positively charged. When you remove the cap, all the positively charged hairs stand up and move as far away as possible from the other positively charged hairs. Two objects that have the same charge push away, or repel, each other.

The negatively charged balloon makes part of the paper positive. That part of the paper pulls toward the balloon.

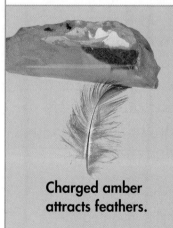

Charged amber attracts feathers.

The Name "Electricity"

Millions of years ago sap oozed from a tree trunk. Gradually the sap hardened. Sometimes it trapped prehistoric insects. Amber is fossilized tree sap. In Greece, a scientist named Thales noticed that amber could do amazing tricks. When amber is rubbed on fur, it becomes charged. Feathers stick to it. The word *electricity* comes from *elektron*, the Greek word for amber.

An Electric Field

The space around electrically charged objects is called an electric field. To represent an electric field, scientists draw lines coming out of an object. An electric field is invisible. It is strongest close to the charged object. It gets weaker farther from the object.

An electric field causes an electric force on charged objects that touch it. A positive electric field attracts negative charges. It pushes away positive charges. A negative electric field attracts positive charges and pushes away negative ones.

The balloons have the same charge. They repel each other.

The balloons have opposite charges. They attract each other.

✓ Lesson Checkpoint

1. What effect will a charged object have on an object with the opposite charge?
2. Give two examples of static electricity.
3. **Writing** in Science **Narrative** Write a story in your **science journal** that tells a curious first grader about static electricity. Include at least two experiences you might have in a typical day.

How do electric charges flow?

How does the electrical energy in a battery get to a light bulb?
To study how electricity moves, scientists build models called circuits.
Electric charges travel through different materials at different speeds.

How Electric Charges Move

Static electricity stays in one place. But most electricity is on the go. An electric charge in motion is called an **electric current.** The electric charge flows from one place to another. An electric current travels quickly and invisibly.

Learning how electricity works can be extremely dangerous. Studying a model is a much smarter way to learn how charges travel. A model of a circuit is shown on the next page. A circuit is a loop. In order for charges to flow through it, a circuit cannot have any breaks. It must be a closed circuit. In contrast, an open circuit has at least one break that interrupts the flow of electric charges. Scientists use symbols to show different parts of the circuit in diagrams. The diagram and the picture on the next page both show the same circuit.

Going with the Flow

The flow of electric charge is not the same in all materials. Some kinds of atoms become charged more easily than others. Materials made up of such atoms are conductors. The copper wire in the picture and most metals are good conductors. Silver is an excellent conductor of electric charge.

Other materials are made of atoms that do not become charged easily. Electric charge moves through them more slowly. These materials are insulators. Plastic, rubber, glass, and dry wood are good insulators. In the circuit picture, the wire is insulated. This insulation prevents the electric charges from coming in contact with other wires. Different colored insulations help show how complex circuits with many wires are connected.

A Closed Circuit

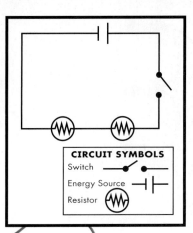

Energy source

Batteries are the power source for this circuit. They cause the electric charges to flow.

Means of Energy Transfer

The wires provide a path through which the charges flow.

Resistor

A coiled wire is inside the light bulb. This wire is made of a material with a high resistance. **Resistance** means the material does not allow electric charges to flow through it easily. Because of this resistance, the flowing electric charges heat up the wire. The wire gives off light.

Switch

When this switch is closed, the circuit is closed. The electric charges flow without any interruptions.

Insulated Wire

The copper wire is insulated with a plastic covering.

1. ✓ **Checkpoint** What is the difference between an insulator and a conductor?

2. 🔄 **Cause and Effect** What causes some materials to be good insulators of electricity?

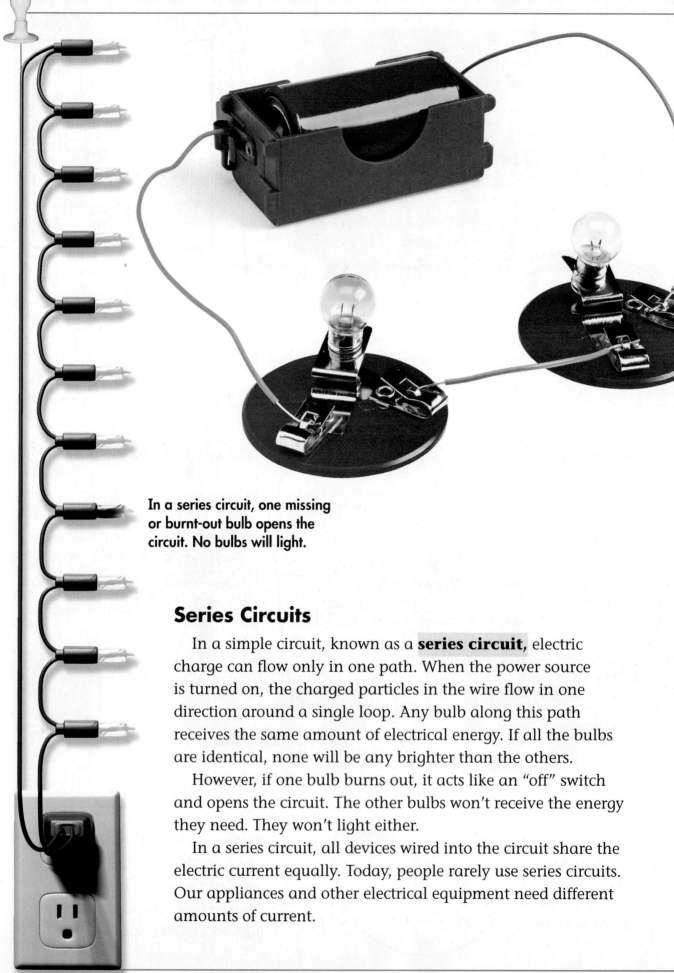

In a series circuit, one missing or burnt-out bulb opens the circuit. No bulbs will light.

Series Circuits

In a simple circuit, known as a **series circuit,** electric charge can flow only in one path. When the power source is turned on, the charged particles in the wire flow in one direction around a single loop. Any bulb along this path receives the same amount of electrical energy. If all the bulbs are identical, none will be any brighter than the others.

However, if one bulb burns out, it acts like an "off" switch and opens the circuit. The other bulbs won't receive the energy they need. They won't light either.

In a series circuit, all devices wired into the circuit share the electric current equally. Today, people rarely use series circuits. Our appliances and other electrical equipment need different amounts of current.

Parallel Circuits

One way to prevent all the lights in a circuit from going out is to connect them in a parallel circuit. A **parallel circuit** has two or more paths for the electric charge to follow. The main loop leaves from and returns to the power source. Along the loop, however, there are little loops. Each little loop is a separate path for the electric charge. How the charges flow through each little loop does not affect the flow of charges in any other path.

Circuits in your home, school, and other buildings are parallel circuits. A break in one part of the circuit does not stop the charge from flowing. Unlike a series circuit, a parallel circuit can handle electrical devices that require different amounts of current.

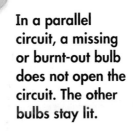

In a parallel circuit, a missing or burnt-out bulb does not open the circuit. The other bulbs stay lit.

✓ Lesson Checkpoint

1. What is the main difference between a series circuit and a parallel circuit?
2. Why are most homes wired in a parallel circuit rather than a series circuit?
3. Art in Science Make a drawing of a parallel circuit that has light bulbs on several little loops. On one of the little loops, draw the light bulbs connected in a series circuit.

381

What are magnetic fields?

Sometimes magnets pull together, but sometimes they push apart. What causes magnets and certain other materials to behave this way?

Magnetism

A magnet is anything that attracts other things made of iron, steel, and certain other metals. **Magnetism** is a force that acts on moving electric charge and magnetic materials that are near a magnet. The word *magnet* comes from Magnesia, a part of ancient Greece that today is part of Turkey. Long ago, Magnesia was famous for having large amounts of lodestone, a magnetic mineral.

Magnetic Fields

How do magnets work? Each magnet has an invisible field around it. The **magnetic field** goes out in all directions. The shape of the magnetic field depends on the shape of the magnet. Look at the patterns of iron filings near the horseshoe magnet and the bar magnets. The patterns are different because the magnetic fields have different shapes. But whatever the shape of the magnet, the field is strongest at the magnet's ends or poles. The pulling or pushing force is strongest at the poles.

Iron filings near a horsehoe magnet show that the magnetic field is strongest near the poles.

Magnetic Poles

All magnets have two poles, a north-seeking and a south-seeking pole. Opposite poles behave in the same way as opposite charges. Unlike charges attract each other, while like charges repel each other. So, the north-seeking pole on one magnet and the south-seeking pole on another magnet attract each other. But the like poles repel.

If you break a magnet into two pieces, you will have two magnets, each with its own north-seeking pole and south-seeking pole. In fact, every magnet has both a north-seeking pole and a south-seeking pole. Think of the two poles of a magnet like two sides of a coin. One cannot exist without the other.

1. ✔ Checkpoint If you break a magnet into two pieces, what happens to its magnetic poles?
2. Social Studies in Science Use the Internet or other resources to locate places other than Magnesia where lodestone is found.

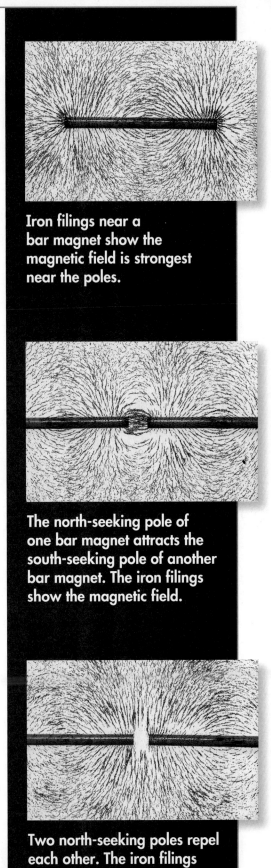

Iron filings near a bar magnet show the magnetic field is strongest near the poles.

The north-seeking pole of one bar magnet attracts the south-seeking pole of another bar magnet. The iron filings show the magnetic field.

Two north-seeking poles repel each other. The iron filings show the magnetic field.

The Largest Magnet in the World

Why does a compass needle always move to the north-south? Many ancient sailors used compasses successfully but didn't know why they worked. Christopher Columbus used a compass when he crossed the Atlantic. Around 1600, English scientist William Gilbert suggested that the world's largest magnet is Earth! In other words, he proposed that Earth is a huge magnet, surrounded by an enormous magnetic field.

Earth behaves like a large magnet. Like all magnets, its magnetic field is strongest at the poles. But Earth's magnetic poles are not located at its geographic poles. The geographic poles are on Earth's axis, an invisible line around which our planet rotates. The magnetic north pole is located in Canada, about 1,000 kilometers (600 miles) from the geographic North Pole. The magnetic south pole is located in the Southern Ocean near Antarctica.

Why does Earth act like a magnet? Scientists aren't sure of the answer. After all, no one has actually seen the inside of our planet. But based on indirect evidence, they suggest that Earth's outer core is made of iron that is so hot that it has melted. As Earth rotates, electric currents that flow in this liquid iron create a magnetic field. The inner core is probably solid iron that is also very hot. It doesn't melt because of the extremely high pressure.

If no magnet is near, the compass needle points north.

A bar magnet changes the direction in which the compass needle points.

How Compasses Work

A compass is a helpful, easy-to-carry tool. Wherever you are on Earth, one end of a compass needle will point to the North Pole. It follows an imaginary line that connects the magnetic poles of Earth. Once you know which direction is north, you can easily determine south, west, and east.

For a compass to work properly, its needle must be lightweight and turn easily. The compass cannot be close to a magnet. Otherwise, the needle will respond to the pull of the magnet rather than to Earth's magnetic field.

The Northern Lights

At certain times of the year, sky-watchers see a spectacular light show called the Aurora Borealis, or the Northern Lights. Auroras are caused by charged particles traveling quickly from the Sun. The charged particles are attracted to the strongest parts of Earth's magnetic field—the magnetic north and south poles. The particles collide with gases in Earth's atmosphere. Atoms in the gases give off the colorful light. Earth is not the only planet with auroras. Astronomers have observed auroras in Jupiter's atmosphere.

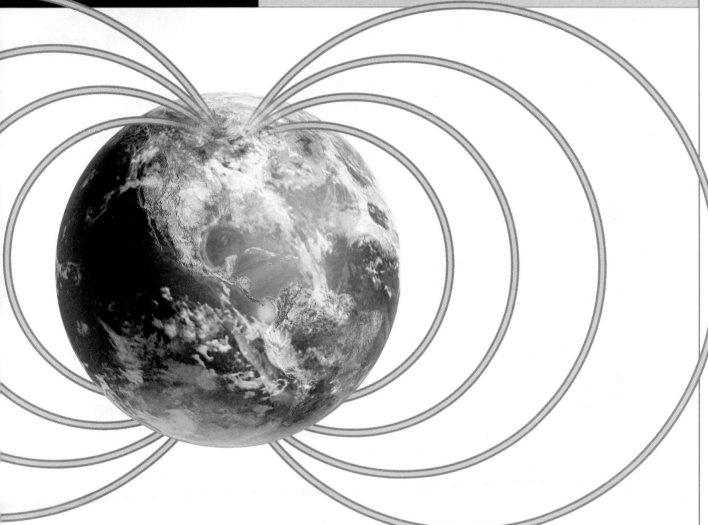

Earth is like a giant magnet surrounded by a huge magnetic field.

✓ Lesson Checkpoint

1. What are some ways that Earth is like a magnet?
2. Why does a compass needle point in a north-south direction?
3. **Writing** in Science **Expository** Compasses can be used to create treasure hunts. Hide a small object. Then write clues on index cards. Hide all but the first clue, which tells how to use a compass to find the next clue, and so on. Challenge a friend to use your directions to find the hidden object.

Lesson 4

How is electricity transformed to magnetism?

Electricity and magnetism are closely related. Both are the result of charged particles moving. The combination of these forces, electromagnetism, is very useful in our daily lives.

Electromagnets

In 1820, Danish scientist Hans Christian Oersted was showing how electric current flowed through a wire. He noticed that the magnetic needle on a nearby compass moved each time he turned on the current. The electric current caused a magnetic field. The current caused the compass needle to move. Oersted saw that the forces of electricity and magnetism have a lot in common. This connection led to an important invention—the electromagnet.

The compass needles line up with the magnetic field caused by the flowing current.

When no current flows, all compasses point north.

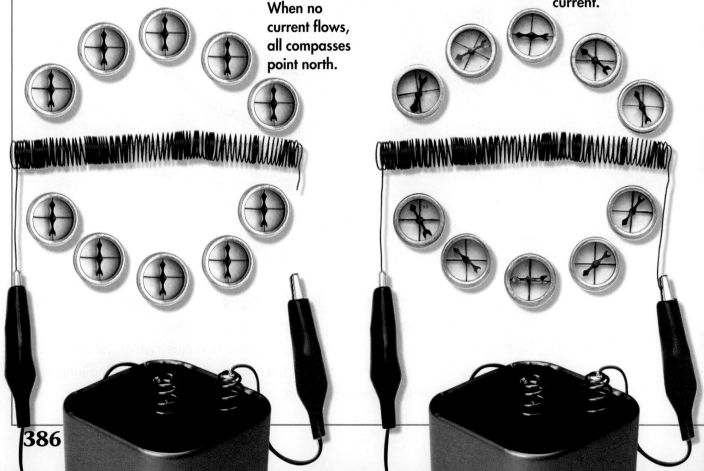

An **electromagnet** is a coil of wire with many loops through which an electric current passes. To make the field even stronger, the coil is often wrapped around an iron core. When the current moves through the wire, an invisible force surrounds the electromagnet. The force is a magnetic field. When the current stops, the wire loses its magnetism. By transforming electrical energy into magnetic energy, an electromagnet can become a very powerful magnet.

More current passing through the wire makes the electromagnet stronger.

More coils make the electromagnet stronger.

A larger core makes the electromagnet stronger.

Ways to Make the Magnet Stronger

Like a bar magnet, an electromagnet has a north and south pole. One advantage electromagnets have over natural ones is that you can change their strength. You can make an electromagnet stronger by increasing the amount of current running through the wire. Another way is by increasing the number of coils. A third way to boost the power of an electromagnet is by making the magnetic core larger.

1. ✓ Checkpoint How is an electromagnet different from a magnet?
2. Math in Science An electromagnet with 12 coils can pick up 4 thumbtacks. You want to make the electromagnet stronger by adding coils. Predict how many coils you need to pick up 5 thumbtacks.

Uses for Electromagnets

Electromagnets are used in industry to lift heavy materials. Sometimes the materials are the resources needed for manufacturing. Sometimes they are waste materials that are being moved so that they can be used in a different way. Electromagnets are also in complex machines used by doctors and scientists.

You may not realize that electromagnets are part of many electronic gadgets that you use every day. Televisions, fans, VCRs, computers, and DVD players all work because of electromagnets. In the examples here—a doorbell, a motor, and earphones—you'll see how electromagnets help convert electric energy to magnetic energy to mechanical energy.

How a Doorbell Works

Button—Pressing the button closes the electric circuit. Current flows to the...

Transformer—This device controls the amount of current that is sent to the...

Electromagnet—Electricity flowing in the coil of wire magnetizes the electromagnet. This pulls up the...

Contact Arm—The arm is attached to a metal clapper that hits the...

Bell—This makes the sound.

Simple Electric Motor

A motor uses magnets to create motion. A simple motor has six parts.

Battery—power source

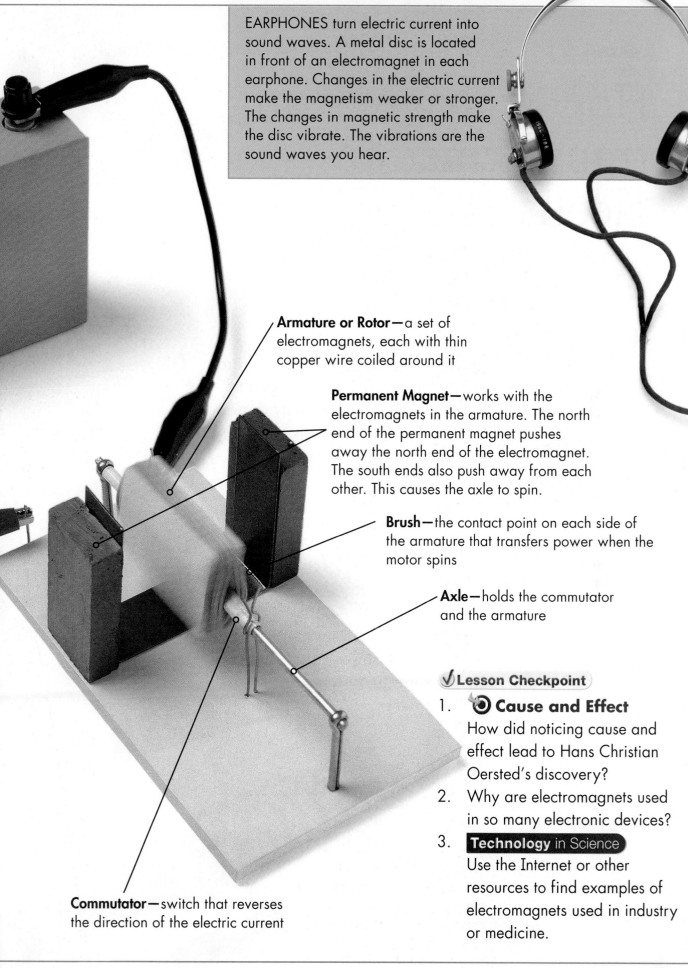

EARPHONES turn electric current into sound waves. A metal disc is located in front of an electromagnet in each earphone. Changes in the electric current make the magnetism weaker or stronger. The changes in magnetic strength make the disc vibrate. The vibrations are the sound waves you hear.

Armature or Rotor—a set of electromagnets, each with thin copper wire coiled around it

Permanent Magnet—works with the electromagnets in the armature. The north end of the permanent magnet pushes away the north end of the electromagnet. The south ends also push away from each other. This causes the axle to spin.

Brush—the contact point on each side of the armature that transfers power when the motor spins

Axle—holds the commutator and the armature

Commutator—switch that reverses the direction of the electric current

✓ **Lesson Checkpoint**

1. 🔄 **Cause and Effect**
   How did noticing cause and effect lead to Hans Christian Oersted's discovery?

2. Why are electromagnets used in so many electronic devices?

3. **Technology** in Science
   Use the Internet or other resources to find examples of electromagnets used in industry or medicine.

Lesson 5

How is magnetism transformed to electricity?

The power of magnetism can be transformed into the power of electricity. This discovery led to the invention of the electric motor, generator, and more.

Electrical Energy

Most people take electricity for granted. They find it hard to picture daily life before electricity. They push plugs into outlets, without thinking about where the electricity comes from. They don't realize that the electrical energy that powers their televisions, refrigerators, and lamps has traveled a long way.

Today we know more ways to use magnetism to generate electricity. Sliding coiled wire back and forth over a magnet generates electricity. Spinning a coiled wire around a magnet produces electricity too.

When a magnet is moved, its magnetic field moves with it. And changing a magnetic field generates electricity. The faster the coiled wire or the magnet is moved, the stronger the electric current it produces. In contrast, the slower the movement, the weaker the current. The number of coiled loops also affects the strength of the current. More coiled loops of wire mean the magnet creates a stronger current.

Wires are wound in coils around magnets. The wires are attached to instruments that measure the electric current.

390

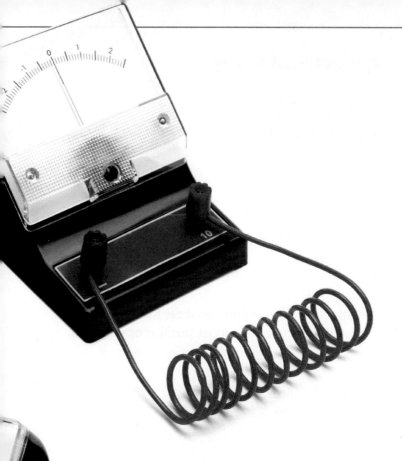

Joseph
Henry

Michael
Faraday

A Flashlight Without Batteries

In 1831, Michael Faraday invented a machine that used magnets to transform motion into an electric current. By turning a crank, he was able to produce electrical energy. He called this invention a dynamo. Today this technology is used in an emergency flashlight. It does not use batteries. Instead, it produces electricity when the user squeezes the handle.

Currents Currently

Most homes, schools, and businesses today get their electricity from generators. A generator is a machine that creates electric energy by turning coils of wire around powerful magnets. Modern generators are much bigger than the magnets and coils that Faraday and other scientists used in their experiments. The basic scientific principles, however, are the same. A generator uses magnets and wires to turn mechanical energy into electrical energy.

Pioneers in Electricity

In the early 1820s, British scientist Michael Faraday did many experiments with magnetism and electricity. At the same time, American scientist Joseph Henry was doing similar experiments. In 1829, Henry discovered that changing a magnetic field created an electric current in a wire. But, he didn't share his findings with other scientists for several years. In 1831, Faraday made the same discovery and shared it with other scientists. Faraday moved a magnet inside a wire coil to generate electrical energy. He used this discovery to build the first electric motor.

1. ✓ **Checkpoint** What happens when a magnet is moved back and forth inside a coiled wire?

2. **Math** in Science How many years after Joseph Henry discovered that changing a magnetic field generates an electric current did Michael Faraday make the same discovery?

Discoveries in Using Electrical Energy

 **600 B.C.** Thales of Miletus and others describe static electricity.

 **1600** William Gilbert suggests that Earth is a magnet.

1740s Benjamin Franklin and Ebenezer Kinnersley describe electric charges as positive or negative.

 **1820** Hans Christian Oersted notices that electric currents affect a compass needle.

1829 1831 Joseph Henry (1829) and Michael Faraday (1831) produce a current by changing a magnetic field.

 **1870** Zenobe Gramme improves the electric generator to make it more powerful.

 **1879** Thomas Edison demonstrates the incandescent light bulb.

 **1884** Charles Parsons develops the first successful steam turbine.

1896 Electric generator at Niagara Falls begins producing electricity for Buffalo, New York.

1980 Windfarms in the United States begin collecting the wind's energy.

How Generators Are Powered

There are many ways for a generator to produce electrical energy. Some use the energy of the wind, while others rely on falling water. Still other generators are powered by steam caused by the hot temperatures deep below Earth's surface or by nuclear energy heating the water. In each kind of generator, mechanical energy spins wires around a magnet.

Wind Power
A wind turbine changes the energy of the blowing wind into electricity.

Hydroelectric Power
The power of falling water is changed into electricity by generators near Niagara Falls.

Electrical Safety

Electricity lights homes, cooks food, and powers many machines. However, if you're not careful, electricity can cause a serious shock or start a fire.

The Electrical Safety Foundation urges everyone to remember the 4 Rs of electrical safety:

- Respect the power of electricity.
- Read and follow the instructions that come with every electrical product.
- Replace worn or cracked electrical cords.
- Relocate, or move, appliance cords so people will not walk on or trip over them, and children or pets can't pull them.

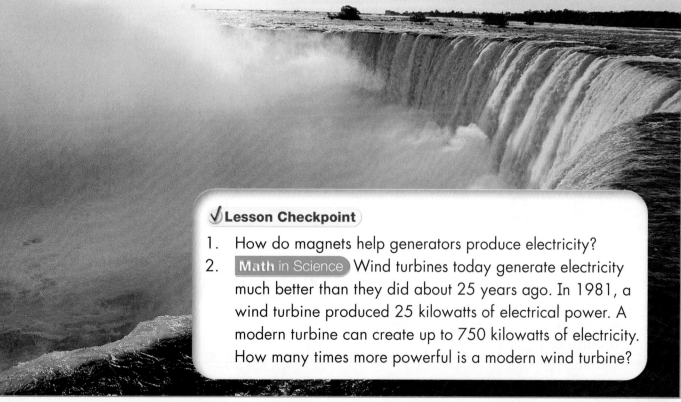

✓ Lesson Checkpoint

1. How do magnets help generators produce electricity?
2. **Math in Science** Wind turbines today generate electricity much better than they did about 25 years ago. In 1981, a wind turbine produced 25 kilowatts of electrical power. A modern turbine can create up to 750 kilowatts of electricity. How many times more powerful is a modern wind turbine?

Investigate What is an electromagnet?

Observe how an electromagnet works. Then make an operational definition. An **operational definition** of an electromagnet is a definition that tells you what you must observe to know if something *is* an electromagnet. Use this form: "An object is an electromagnet if it acts like a magnet when _____, but not when _____."

Materials

safety goggles and ruler

insulated wire and bolt

battery and battery holder

20 small paper clips

What to Do

1 Start 25 centimeters from one end of the wire. Coil the wire 30 times around the bolt near its head.

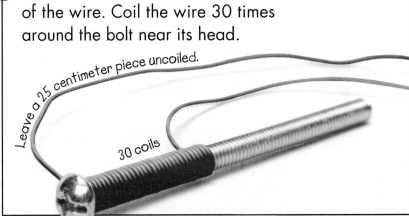

Leave a 25 centimeter piece uncoiled.

30 coils

2 Hold the bolt's head near a paper clip. Record your **observations**.

Be careful!

Wear safety goggles. Disconnect wires if any parts feel warm.

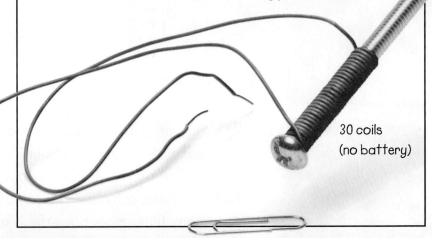

30 coils (no battery)

Process Skills

You use your experience with an object or event to help make an **operational definition** of it.

3 Make a circuit. Put a battery in the battery holder. Attach both ends of the wire to it. Find how many paper clips your electromagnet can pick up. Record. Then remove a wire from the battery holder.

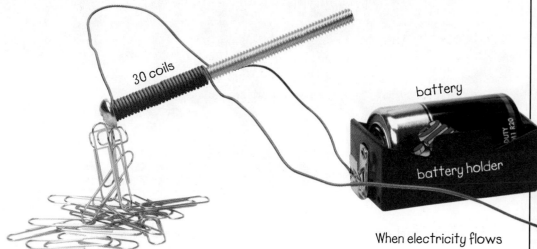

30 coils

battery

battery holder

When electricity flows through the wire, the bolt works like a magnet.

4 Add 20 more coils. **Predict** how many paper clips you can pick up now. Find out.

5 Make a bar graph or select another way to show your results.

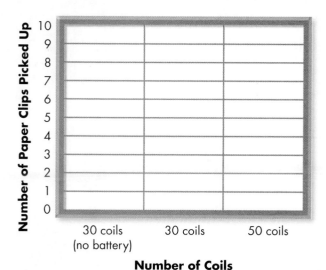

Number of Paper Clips Picked Up

10
9
8
7
6
5
4
3
2
1
0

30 coils (no battery)   30 coils   50 coils

Number of Coils

Number of Coils	Number of Paper Clips Picked Up
30 coils (no battery)	
30 coils	
50 coils	

Explain Your Results

1. **Infer** What can make an electromagnet stronger?

2. Make an **operational definition** of an electromagnet.

Go Further

Which objects will a magnet attract? Use your electromagnet as a tool. Develop and carry out a plan to answer this or another question you may have. Write instructions others could use to repeat your investigation.

395

Using Numbers to Represent Electrical Charges

Positive and negative numbers are often used in science. Numbers greater than zero are positive, and numbers less than zero are negative. Positive numbers can be written without a sign. So "positive five" can be written as +5 or 5. You have worked with positive and negative temperatures. You can also use positive and negative numbers to represent electrical charges.

When a neutral material loses particles with negative charges, it has a positive charge. An opposite charge makes it neutral again. If the charge is +5, a charge of −5 will make it neutral again.

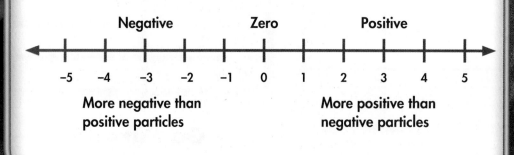

Negative   Zero   Positive

−5 −4 −3 −2 −1   0   1   2   3   4   5

More negative than positive particles   More positive than negative particles

Use the number line to answer these questions.

1. If some material has a charge of +4, what charge would make it neutral?
   A. +2
   B. –2
   C. +4
   D. –4

2. If a neutral balloon gains 3 negative charges and then loses 3 negative charges, what will its charge be?
   F. +3
   G. –3
   H. 0
   I. +6

3. If a balloon with a negative charge and a balloon with a positive charge are held up by strings next to each other, what will happen?
   A. They will move toward each other.
   B. They will move apart.
   C. Nothing will happen.
   D. They will both fall to the floor.

Lab zone Take-Home Activity

Design an experiment in which you try to stick charged balloons to a variety of objects at home, such as the refrigerator, a door, and so on. Time how long the balloon sticks to each (if it sticks at all). Make a graph that shows your results. Try this experiment in different kinds of weather.

Chapter 13 Review and Test Prep

Use Vocabulary

electric current (p. 378)	**parallel circuit** (p. 381)
electromagnet (p. 387)	**resistance** (p. 379)
magnetic field (p. 382)	**series circuit** (p. 380)
magnetism (p. 382)	**static electricity** (p. 375)

Use the vocabulary term from the list above that best completes each sentence.

1. If charged particles in an object are not balanced, the object builds up _____.

2. A charge in motion is called a(n) _____.

3. _____ is the pushing or pulling force that exists when a magnetic material is near.

4. Current flows in only one direction in a(n) _____.

5. The quality of _____ opposes the flow of electric current through a material.

6. Because of Earth's _____, a compass needle points in a north-south direction.

7. One advantage of a(n) _____ over a natural magnet is that its magnetic field can be turned off.

8. A(n) _____ can handle appliances that use different amounts of electric current.

Explain Concepts

9. Explain why copper wire is a better conductor of electricity than a rubber tube is.

10. Explain why most homes have parallel circuits rather than series circuits.

Process Skills

11. **Predict** A compass needle is pointing north-south. What would happen to the needle if a small magnet were held near the east side of the compass?

12. **Infer** You rub two inflated balloons on your hair. What happens when you hold them close to each other?

13. **Ask a question** If you were able to interview either Joseph Henry or Michael Faraday about his experiments with electricity, what two questions would you ask?

 Cause and Effect

14. Complete the graphic organizer to show cause and effect for the Northern Lights.

Cause		Effect
	→	The particles collide with gases in Earth's atmosphere.

Cause		Effect
The particles collide with gases in Earth's atmosphere.	→	

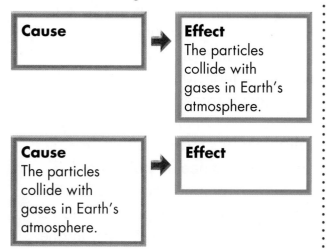

Test Prep

15. Which of the following is NOT used to power generators?
  Ⓐ wind
  Ⓑ moving water
  Ⓒ hot rocks deep below Earth's surface
  Ⓓ static electricity

16. Lights are wired in a parallel circuit. What happens to the circuit if one bulb burns out?
  Ⓕ None of the bulbs light.
  Ⓖ Half of the bulbs light.
  Ⓗ All bulbs but one light.
  Ⓘ All bulbs light.

17. If you break a magnet into two pieces, what happens?
  Ⓐ The magnetic field disappears until the pieces are put back together.
  Ⓑ Each magnet piece has only one magnetic pole.
  Ⓒ Each magnet piece has a north pole and a south pole.
  Ⓓ One magnet piece has two north poles and the other has two south poles.

18. Which of the following materials would be the best insulator for a metal wire?
  Ⓕ glass
  Ⓖ silver
  Ⓗ water
  Ⓘ copper

19. Explain why the answer you chose for Question 18 is the best. For each answer you did not select, give a reason why it is not the best choice.

20. Writing in Science **Expository**
Suppose you are asked to give a speech to a third-grade class that explains the 4 Rs of electrical safety. Write your speech.

William Gilbert

William Gilbert is an important person in the history of electricity and magnetism. He studied at St. John's College of Cambridge University in England. In 1569, he graduated and became a doctor in London. He later served as the doctor for Queen Elizabeth I and King James I.

Electricity and magnetism greatly interested Gilbert. He explained that static electricity and magnetism are different forces. In 1600, he published a book called *On the Magnet.* In this book he described Earth's magnetic field. He explained that a compass needle points north-south because Earth is a giant magnet. Gilbert also developed and conducted experiments to test his ideas about electricity and magnetism. In one of these experiments, he discovered that heating magnets changed their magnetic properties. Magnets placed in a fire lost their magnetism.

William Gilbert introduced a theory about the effect electricity and magnetism have on each other. He was also the first person to use the word *electric* to describe the force between charged objects.

His ideas influenced many scientists after him. Galileo and Johannes Kepler are two famous scientists who studied his work.

Lab zone Take-Home Activity

Benjamin Franklin and Thomas Edison are two scientists who studied electricity. Find out more about them and write what you learn in your science journal.

You Will Discover

- how sound travels.
- some properties of sound.
- what light is.
- how light behaves.

Chapter 14

Sound and Light

online
Student Edition
pearsonsuccessnet.com

How do sound and light travel?

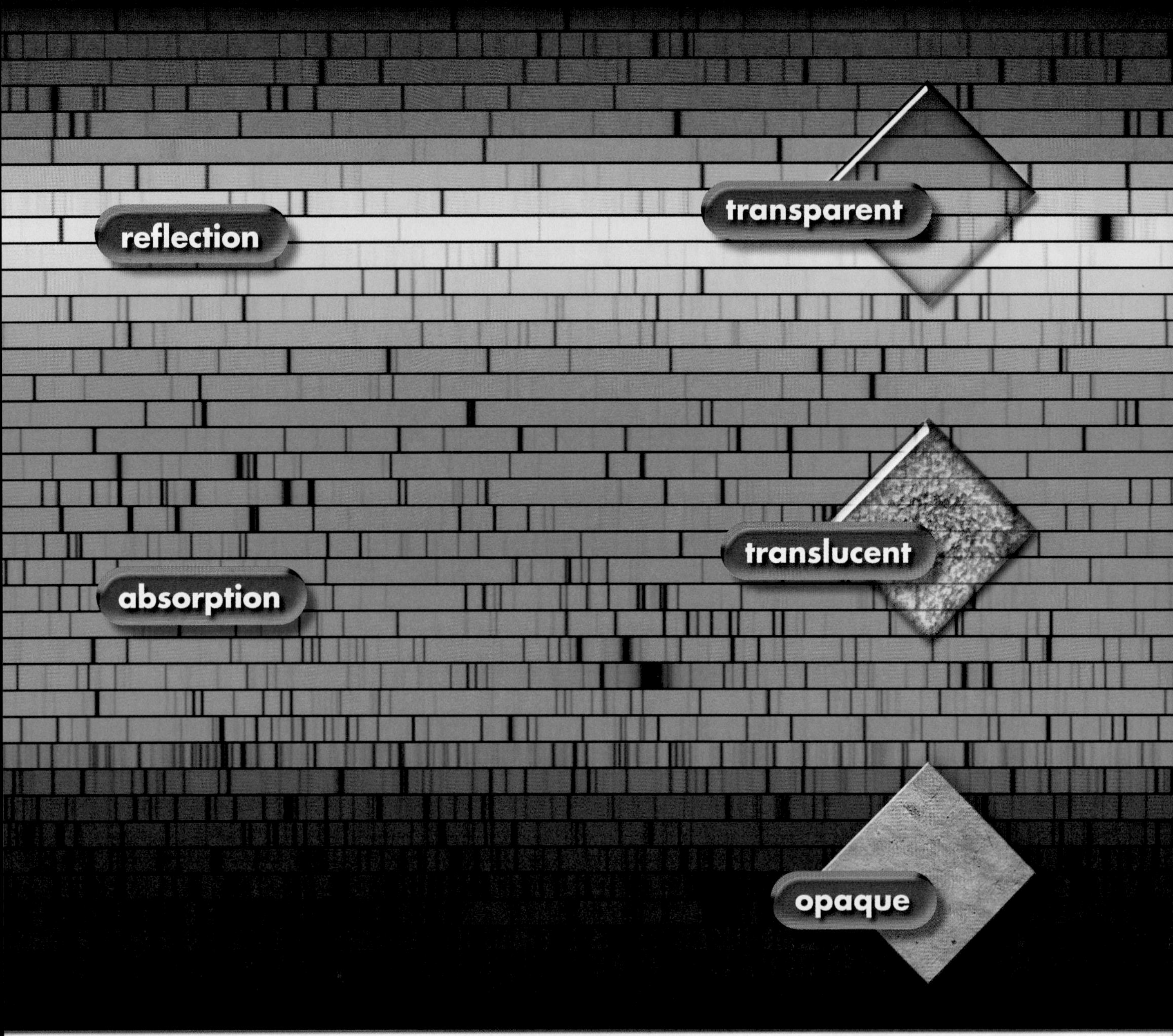

transparent

reflection

translucent

absorption

opaque

frequency   wavelength   compression

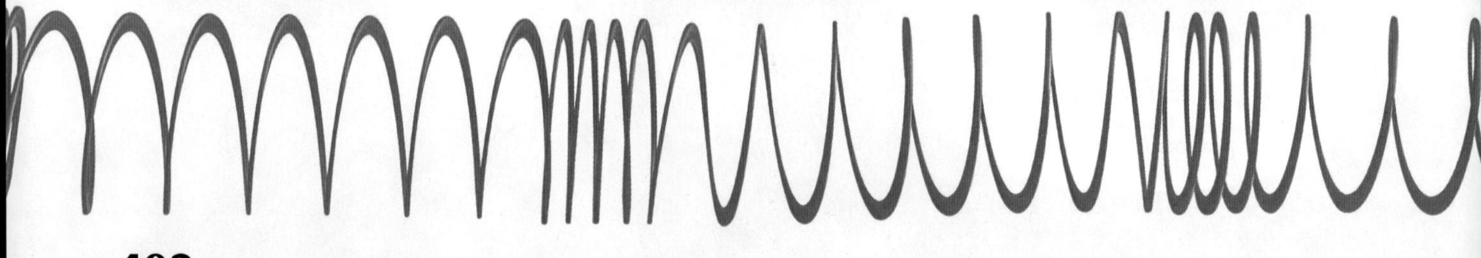

Chapter 14 Vocabulary

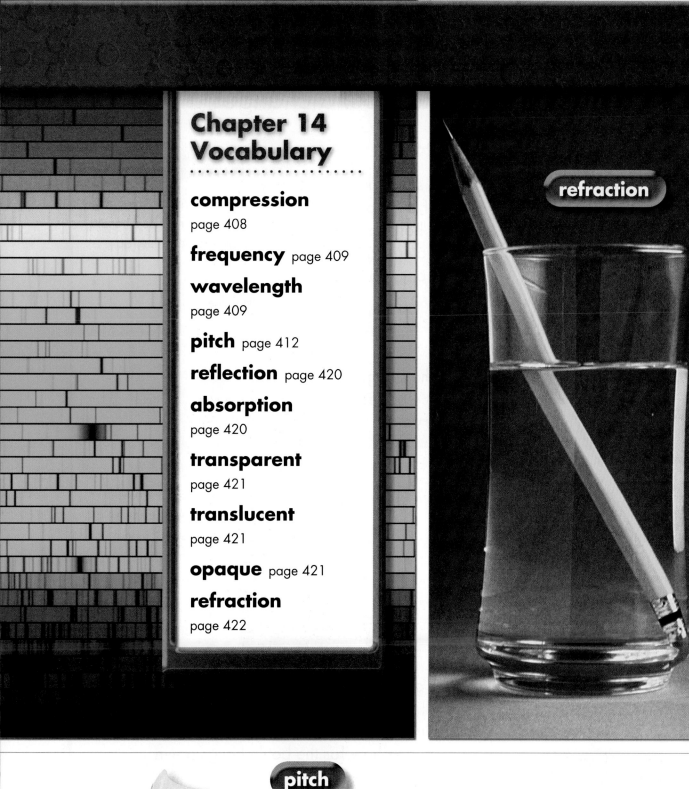

refraction

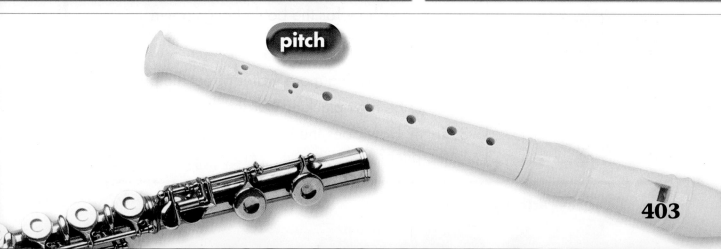

pitch

Explore What makes sound change?

Materials

water

funnel and
2 L plastic bottle
with cap

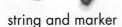

string and marker

What to Do

1 Tie the string around the neck of a 2 L bottle. Fill the bottle about $\frac{1}{3}$ full with water. Screw cap tightly onto bottle.

Use a funnel to add the water.

Tie the string to the marker. Use the marker as a handle. Hold it on the desktop.

Pluck the string here.

2 Pluck the string. Does it vibrate? **Observe** the sound.

Put on lid.

Sound is made when the string vibrates. The faster it vibrates, the higher the pitch.

$\frac{1}{3}$ full of water

almost touching the floor

3 Figure out how the sound changes when you:
  a. fill the bottle with water,
  b. pluck the string gently and hard, and
  c. shorten how far the bottle hangs down.

Explain Your Results

1. How did adding more water affect the pitch?

2. Describe how plucking harder changes volume.

3. **Infer** How does the length of the string affect the pitch?

Draw Conclusions

A **conclusion** is a decision you reach after you think about facts and details. You can also use what you know or observe to **make an inference** or form an opinion about events.

Magazine Article

Fly-by-Night Creatures

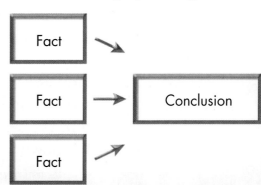

Bats are flying mammals. Many come out at night. They use sounds to help them locate objects in the darkness. The sounds waves travel through the air and bounce off whatever they strike. This creates an echo that travels back to the bat.

The bat can learn many things from the echo. The bat can tell an object's size, direction, distance, and speed. The bat can avoid crashing into an object such as a large tree. If the echo is from a tiny flying insect such as a mosquito or a moth, the bat knows exactly where to catch its dinner. Even blind bats catch their food without flying into things.

Apply It!

Answer the questions by **drawing conclusions** or **making inferences** from the magazine article. Use a graphic organizer like the one shown.

1. You see several bats swooping over a pond at dusk. Why are they doing this?

2. What might a bat conclude from an echo it receives as it flies over the pond?

```
[ Fact ]  →
[ Fact ]  →  [ Conclusion ]
[ Fact ]  →
```

You Are There!

You are standing at the shore of a lake. The water is as smooth as glass. You pick up a rock and toss it into the water. It splashes with a loud "ker-PLUNK" and vanishes—but not without a trace. A ring of ripples spreads out from the spot where your rock plunged into the lake. The outer rings grow bigger. Smaller new rings that form at the center follow them. These ripply rings are waves. Did you know that invisible waves are all around us? Lots of good things come to us in waves: sunlight, music, and even your favorite TV show!

What is sound energy?

Sound is a form of energy that travels in waves. All sounds have common characteristics that can be measured and described. Sound can travel through solids, liquids, and gases.

What Sound Is

The blare of an alarm clock, the beep of a car horn, the quack of a duck, and the rumble of thunder during a storm are all sounds. Sound is a form of energy. Sounds occur when objects vibrate. A vibration is a kind of wiggle. It is a quick back-and-forth movement.

For example, if you pluck a guitar string, the string will vibrate. The vibrating string passes energy to the air that surrounds it, so the air vibrates too. The vibrations travel through the air as sound waves. A sound wave is a disturbance that moves energy through matter. Sound waves carry sound energy. If the waves reach our ears, we hear the sound made by the guitar string.

1. ✓**Checkpoint** What is sound?
2. **Writing in Science** **Descriptive** In your **science journal,** write a paragraph that describes one sound you like to hear and one sound you do not like to hear. Explain what qualities in a sound make you like it or dislike it.

Types of Sound Waves

As sound waves move, they set air particles into motion. The moving air particles form a pattern. Areas with groups of particles that are bunched together alternate with areas of particles that are far apart. The part of the wave where the particles are bunched together is called a **compression.**

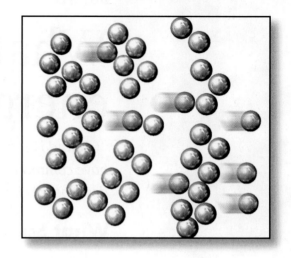

Scientists classify waves according to the way they travel through matter. There are two major types of waves.

Transverse Waves

You are probably familiar with one type of wave. Suppose you and a friend hold opposite ends of a jump rope. You allow some slack so the middle of the rope dips toward the ground. With a quick upward flick of your wrist you send energy through the rope. The disturbance, or wave, moves through the rope to your friend's hand. However, the rope only moves, or vibrates, up and down. You created transverse waves.

In a transverse wave, the particles in the material move at a right angle to the direction that the wave travels. In other words, the wave traveled forward, toward your friend. However, the rope moved up and down. Sometimes waves in a lake or an ocean are transverse waves.

Longitudinal Waves

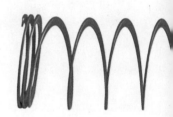

In a longitudinal wave, the particles in the material move parallel to the direction the wave travels. If the wave moves from right to left, then the particles also vibrate from right to left.

A spring toy can help you understand how longitudinal waves move. Suppose you lay the toy on the floor and stretch it slightly. You hold one end and your friend holds the other. Suppose you pull on the end and then push it in. You send energy through the spring. Vibrations pass along the toy. Some of the coils crowd closer together. Then, after the vibrations pass, the coils move farther apart. Sound waves are longitudinal waves. A sound wave travels as air particles are pushed together and then move apart.

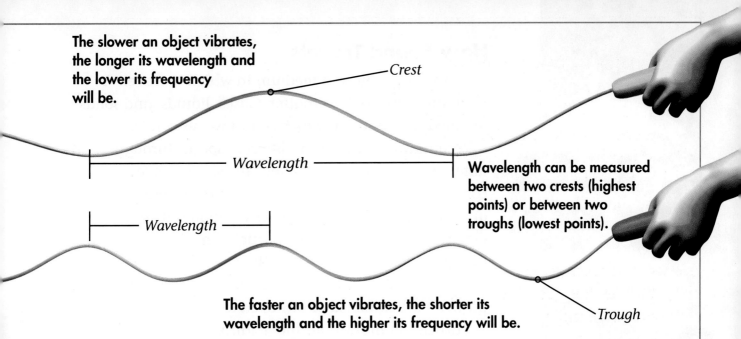

The slower an object vibrates, the longer its wavelength and the lower its frequency will be.

Crest

Wavelength

Wavelength can be measured between two crests (highest points) or between two troughs (lowest points).

Wavelength

The faster an object vibrates, the shorter its wavelength and the higher its frequency will be.

Trough

Frequency and Wavelength

Waves travel in different ways. They can carry different amounts of energy. But, all waves have certain properties. Frequency and wavelength are two of those properties.

The **frequency** of a wave is the number of waves that pass a point in a certain amount of time. The faster an object vibrates, the higher its frequency will be. Frequency is often described as the number of complete cycles a wave makes in one second. A cycle is a vibration.

Most sounds consist of sound waves of several frequencies. **Wavelength** is the distance between a point on one wave and a similar point on the next wave.

Compression

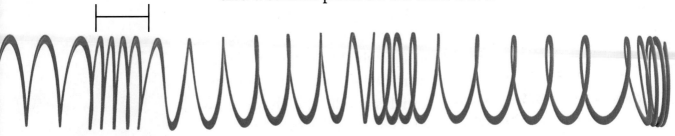

Wavelength is the distance from a compression to the next compression.

1. ✓ Checkpoint What are two types of waves?
2. Health in Science The unit used to measure sound frequency is the hertz. One cycle per second equals one hertz. A person with normal hearing can hear sounds in the frequency range of 20 to 20,000 hertz. People older than 70, however, cannot always hear sounds above 6,000 hertz. Do they have trouble hearing high-frequency or low-frequency sounds?

How Sound Travels

Sound waves need a medium in which to travel. A medium is any kind of matter. Gases, liquids, and solids are mediums through which sound waves can travel.

A sound wave travels at different speeds through different mediums. As it travels, the sound wave compresses the particles in the medium. Several causes affect how fast the sound moves through a medium. One cause is how much the particles move in response to a vibration and how easily they move back to their original position. Another cause is how strongly the particles are attached or attracted to each other.

Particles in most solids move fairly quickly in response to a sound vibration. They also bounce back fairly quickly from the compression. The vibration passes quickly through the particles of most solids. The particles in solids are also fairly strongly attracted to each other. So a sound wave passes quickly.

In most liquids, particles tend to move a little less quickly and bounce back less easily than in a solid. The particles of a liquid are not attracted as strongly to each other as those in a solid. So sound waves tend to travel more slowly in a liquid medium than in most solids.

In a gas such as air, sound waves travel most slowly. The particles of a gas are not attracted to each other as strongly as the particles in a liquid. They are not compressed easily by sound. They also do not bounce back very easily. So sound waves travel slowly.

If you were floating in outer space, you would be in complete silence. Space is a vacuum—an empty place that contains no matter. Since there are no particles of matter in a vacuum, sound waves would not be able to travel to your ears.

Solid

Liquid

Gas

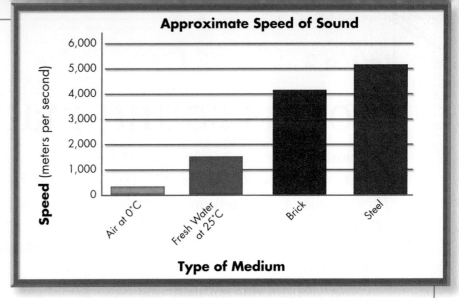

Approximate Speed of Sound

Speed (meters per second)

6,000	
5,000	
4,000	
3,000	
2,000	
1,000	
0	

Air at 0°C · Fresh Water at 25°C · Brick · Steel

Type of Medium

Scientists use echoes to map the ocean floor.

Echoes

As a sound wave travels, it often bumps into objects. If it hits a hard, smooth surface, the wave reflects. That means that the sound bounces back. For example, if you shout your name into a cave, you will hear your name softly repeated. The sound waves bounced off the cave walls and traveled back to you. A reflected sound is called an echo.

Scientists use sound waves to learn about the bottom of the ocean. The sound waves travel down, hit the ocean floor, and return to the surface as echoes. By measuring the total time that passes between sending the sound wave and receiving the echo, scientists can figure out how deep the ocean is there.

✔ Lesson Checkpoint

1. Why does sound travel fastest in solids and slowest in gases?
2. How does an echo form?
3. **⊙ Draw Conclusions** A bird perched in a tree hears the chirping of another bird. A whale hears the songlike sound made by another whale swimming near it. Which sound travels faster, the bird's chirping or the whale's singing? Explain how you decided.

411

How is sound made?

Vibrating objects produce all types of sound. The way an object is made and the way it vibrates affect the type of sound we hear. The frequency and the amount of energy in the sound wave also affect the sound we hear.

Loudness

When you describe a sound, one of the first things you think about is loudness. You whisper around a sleeping baby, but you might give an ear-splitting shout when your favorite baseball player hits a home run. Your shout is a lot louder than the whisper, but what exactly is loudness? Loudness is a measure of how strong a sound seems to us. Loudness is related to the amount of energy in a sound wave.

If you are far from the source of a sound, it will not sound as loud as if you were standing nearer to it. Suppose you are sitting next to a friend who is playing the drums. The sound waves do not have far to travel to your ears, so they will sound loud. But if you were across the street, the sound of the drums would be softer. The sound waves do not lose some of their energy as they travel through the air. The energy just spreads out to cover a larger area, like waves on a pond.

Loudness of Sound

Whisper

Alarm clock

Rock music

Jet

Soft ➡ Loud

Pitch

Another characteristic of sound is pitch. **Pitch** is what makes a sound seem high or low. Pitch depends on a sound's frequency. Objects that vibrate quickly, those with high frequencies, have a high pitch. Objects that vibrate slowly have a low frequency and a low pitch. The material of the object making the sound and its size and shape affect the sound you hear.

A gong is a percussion instrument. When a person hits a gong, the metal vibrates. Its sound is a blend of pitches.

When a tuning fork is struck, it vibrates at a single frequency. It gives off a pure tone of a certain pitch.

A flute is a wind instrument. When the flute player blows across a hole in the flute, the column of air inside the instrument vibrates.

The violinist rubs the bow across the strings, causing them to vibrate. The strings that play the highest notes are thin metal wires.

1. ✓ **Checkpoint** What type of pitch does a high-frequency sound have?

2. **Social Studies** in Science The sounds from machinery, traffic, construction, and airplanes make noise pollution. Many towns have rules that limit noise levels. Suppose you were part of your local government. Write one rule you would make to keep noise from becoming a problem.

How Instruments Make Sound

Guitars, violins, harps, and other string instruments make sound when a musician plucks, rubs, or hits the strings. This sends vibrations through the instrument.

Strings on a guitar are stretched between the top and bottom of the instrument. A guitarist plays notes by plucking the strings. The note depends on the length and thickness of the string and how tightly it is stretched. A guitarist tunes the guitar by tightening the strings to make the pitch higher or loosening them to make it lower.

Sound waves travel slowest through the thicker, heavier strings. These strings vibrate slowest and play the lowest pitches. Waves travel more quickly through the thinner strings. They vibrate faster and have higher pitches.

To shorten a string and raise its pitch, a musician presses down on the metal frets or bars along the neck of the guitar.

The longer recorder has a lower pitch than the shorter instrument.

Percussion Instruments

Drums, xylophones, and maracas are examples of percussion instruments. Percussion instruments make sounds when you shake or strike them. For example, when you hit a drum with your hand or a stick, the skin across the top of the drum vibrates and produces sound.

Wind Instruments

In a wind instrument such as a recorder, the musician blows across a hole. This causes particles in a column of air inside the instrument to vibrate. The vibrations produce the sound you hear. The shorter the instrument, the shorter the column of air and the higher its pitch will be.

The Piano

A piano has more than 200 strings. Each key on a piano matches a group of strings. When you press a key, a padded hammer strikes the group of strings. The strings vibrate and produce a tone. Pressing a key extra hard will not change either frequency or pitch. But it will make the sound louder.

A tuning key is used to tighten or loosen each string.

Hitting a drum closer to the center lowers the pitch.

The piano has features of both percussion and string instruments.

How We Hear

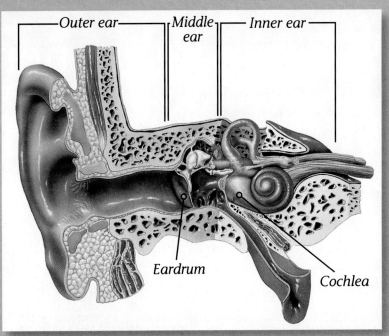

Outer ear — Middle ear — Inner ear

Eardrum

Cochlea

The outer part of the human ear funnels sounds into the ear canal. Inside the ear canal, the sound waves hit the eardrum. The sound waves make the eardrum vibrate. The vibrating eardrum causes three tiny connected bones in the middle ear to vibrate. Because of their shapes, the bones are named the hammer, the stirrup, and the anvil. Next, the vibrations move into the cochlea in the inner ear. The cochlea is a snail-shaped organ that is filled with a liquid. When the liquid in the cochlea starts to vibrate, tiny hairs in the cochlea move. They convert the vibrations into signals that travel along the auditory nerve to the brain. The brain interprets the signals as sound.

✔ Lesson Checkpoint

1. How does a wind instrument produce sound?
2. How does the pitch of a thick guitar string compare with that of a thinner string?
3. **Draw Conclusions** By shortening or tightening a guitar string, you raise the pitch. What do you conclude will happen to the pitch if you tighten the skin stretched across the top of a drum?

energy. Both travel as waves. Only a tiny fraction of light energy can be seen by the human eye.

Sources of Light

Like sound, light is a form of energy. The Sun, a bonfire, a street lamp, and a firefly are just a few sources of light energy.

No light source is more important to us than the Sun. Without a constant supply of energy from the Sun, Earth would be a dead planet. It would be too cold and dark for any kind of life. Plants, for example, convert sunlight into chemical energy, which they use to make food. Plants are part of the food chain. Without plants, animals and people could not survive.

Some animals give off light called bioluminescence. The light is a result of chemical reactions inside the animal's body. Some sea animals that live near the bottom of the ocean—where it is pitch black—are bioluminescent.

Long, long ago, humans discovered that they could make their own light. The discovery of fire opened up a whole new world. No longer did almost all activities have to stop as soon as the Sun went down. People could light a campfire and stay warm, cook food, or work even after dark.

Stick puppets cast their shadows on a screen. The shadows can be made larger by moving the puppets closer to the light source.

The firefly is a bioluminescent insect.

416

The Light Bulb

In the 1870s, American inventor Thomas Edison and British inventor Joseph Swan discovered that electric current would heat up a filament, or thread, until it gave off both heat energy and light energy. They put the filament inside a hollow glass ball. They passed an electric current through the filament. It got very hot. It glowed, but it did not catch fire! This invention was the light bulb.

Thomas Edison demonstrated this type of lamp in the United States in October 1879.

Shadows

Light travels in straight lines called rays that fan outward from the source of the light. You can easily see how light travels by looking at a shadow.

If you hold your hand in front of a wall and then shine a flashlight on it, a hand-shaped shadow will show up on the wall. Your hand blocks the path of the light rays. A shadow, or dark area, appears where the light rays cannot reach the wall. The size of the shadow can change. If you hold your hand very close to the wall and shine the flashlight on it, the shadow will be about the same size as your hand. If you move your hand away from the wall and closer to the flashlight, the shadow will be larger than your hand.

The angle that the light strikes the object also affects the size of the shadow. Think of your own shadow on a sunny day. Around noon, when the Sun is highest in the sky, your shadow is short. Early in the morning or late in the day, the Sun is lower in the sky. Your shadow is longer.

1. **✓Checkpoint** What do the Sun, a bonfire, and a street lamp have in common?
2. **Art** in Science You can put on a shadow puppet play with only a source of light and a darkened room. Use your fingers and hands to form "characters" such as birds, rabbits, and other animals. Write a short script and put on a play for some friends or classmates.

Light Waves We See

The light we can see makes up only a thin slice of the universe's light energy. Scientists refer to all forms of light energy as electromagnetic radiation. Visible light, the light we see, is the most familiar form of electromagnetic waves.

Light energy travels as a wave. Like all waves, light waves have wavelengths and frequencies. The human eye can see only the wavelengths and frequencies of the colors in the visible spectrum. White light, such as light from a lamp or the Sun, is actually a blend of the colors in a rainbow. Sunlight that passes through the raindrops is split into individual colors. The colors are red, orange, yellow, green, blue, and violet.

These colors always appear in the same order because of their wavelength and frequency. As you move from left to right on the spectrum, wavelength decreases and frequency increases. So, red light has the longest wavelength and the lowest frequency. Violet light has the shortest wavelength and the highest frequency.

Electromagnetic Waves We Cannot See

Most of the waves in the electromagnetic spectrum are not visible. Radio waves, microwaves, and infrared waves are invisible because their wavelengths are too long for the human eye to see. Ultraviolet waves, X rays, and gamma rays are high-energy waves. They are invisible because their wavelengths are too short.

Scientists use special equipment to study the invisible waves in the electromagnetic spectrum. These invisible waves behave in the same way as the visible light waves. All electromagnetic waves travel at the same speed through empty space. They all carry energy. This energy can be absorbed by an object and then changed to another form of energy such as heat.

Large amounts of high-energy waves can harm living cells. For example, ultraviolet waves from the Sun can damage the eyes or cause sunburn or cancer. But in smaller amounts, these waves can be helpful. Ultraviolet waves are used to kill bacteria. Microwaves are radio waves that cook or warm food. X rays show doctors such things as a broken bone inside a patient's body.

Red light is at the left end of the spectrum of visible light. It has the longest wavelength and the lowest frequency.

Microwaves passing through food cause particles in it to vibrate quickly. The vibrations produce heat.

418

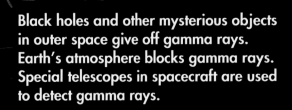

Black holes and other mysterious objects in outer space give off gamma rays. Earth's atmosphere blocks gamma rays. Special telescopes in spacecraft are used to detect gamma rays.

Ultraviolet waves, X rays, and gamma rays have short wavelengths and high frequencies.

Violet light is at the right end of the spectrum of the colors of visible light. It has the shortest wavelength and the highest frequency.

X rays pass through soft body parts such as skin but are absorbed by hard substances such as bone.

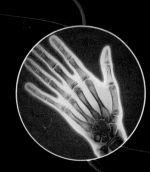

Radio and television stations send out signals on different radio wave frequencies. When you change the channel, you are changing the frequency of the radio wave that your radio or TV receives.

✓ Lesson Checkpoint

1. What colors of light make up the visible spectrum?
2. Why can't humans see X rays?
3. **Draw Conclusions** Laser light waves all have the same wavelength. What can you conclude about the color of laser light?

419

Lesson 4

How do light and matter interact?

Light may behave in different ways when it strikes matter. What happens depends on the type of matter the light waves strike.

Light and Matter

Light rays travel in straight lines—as long as nothing is in their way! But light can change when it strikes an object. The light rays may pass through the object. They may reflect off the object. Or, they may be absorbed by the object.

Light waves reflect at least a little off most objects. **Reflection** occurs when light rays bounce, or reflect, from a surface back to our eyes. Some objects reflect more light rays than others. When you brush your teeth in front of a mirror, the smooth, shiny surface of the mirror reflects almost all the light rays that hit it. The rays reflect back to your eyes at the same angle. You see a clear image, or reflection, of your toothpaste-filled mouth.

Light waves can also be absorbed. **Absorption** occurs when an object takes in the light wave. After a light wave is absorbed, it becomes a form of heat energy.

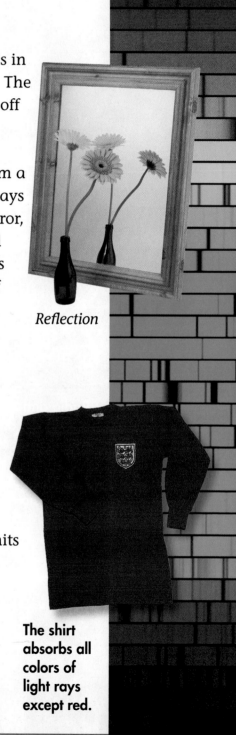

Reflection

Color and Light

We see colors because objects absorb some frequencies of light and reflect others. The shirt at the right looks red because it reflects light rays of the red frequency. It absorbs light rays of other visible color frequencies.

Black and white objects are special cases. When light hits a white T-shirt, for example, all color frequencies in the visible spectrum are reflected. When the colors all blend, they look white. An object looks black because it absorbs all colors of the visible spectrum. On a sunny day, black objects feel warm because the light energy they absorb changes into heat energy.

The shirt absorbs all colors of light rays except red.

Letting Light Through

Materials can be grouped by how they react to light. Materials that transmit nearly all of the light rays that hit them are **transparent.** This means that these materials let the light rays pass through them. You can clearly see what is on the other side of transparent material. Air, clean water, and most windows are transparent. Transparent objects that are colored reflect and transmit only that color. They absorb the other colors. For example, sunglasses that are tinted blue reflect and transmit only blue frequencies. They absorb all others.

Materials that let some light rays pass through but scatter other rays are **translucent.** You can see that light passes through a translucent material, but what is on the other side of it looks blurry. Waxed paper, lampshades, frosted glass, and beeswax are translucent.

Materials that do not let any light pass through are **opaque.** You cannot see through an opaque object. An opaque material either reflects or absorbs the light rays that strike it. Aluminum foil is an example of an opaque material that reflects light. The light bounces off the foil, making the surface look bright and shiny. Wood is an opaque material that absorbs light.

1. ✓Checkpoint How does light behave when it strikes a transparent object?

2. Math in Science Sunglasses help protect the eyes by causing some light rays to be absorbed, scattered, or reflected away from the eyes. A typical pair of sunglasses might transmit $\frac{3}{10}$ of visible light rays. What fraction of visible light do the glasses reflect, scatter, or absorb?

How Light Changes Direction

The light rays refract, or bend, as they travel from the pencil to water to glass to air. That's why the pencil looks broken.

Light can be transmitted, reflected, and absorbed, but that's not all. Light can also be bent!

Unlike sound, light does not need a medium to travel through. In fact, light travels fastest through the emptiness of a vacuum such as outer space. Light slows a little when it travels through various mediums. Light travels more slowly in a gas such as air than in a vacuum. So, a light wave that travels from a vacuum to a gas slows down when it hits the gas.

Particles in a liquid are closer together than the particles in a gas. So, light travels through a liquid more slowly than through a gas. Light moves most slowly through the tightly packed particles in solids.

When light moves at an angle from one medium to another, some of the light is reflected, some is absorbed, and some passes through and changes directions. It bends! This bending is called **refraction.** As a light ray moves at an angle from one transparent medium to another, it changes speed. The change in speed causes the light to refract, or bend. In white light that is separated into individual colors, each color bends differently. The longer the color's wavelength, the less it bends. The picture of the pencil shows what happens when light travels from the pencil through water, through a glass, then through the air to your eye.

SciLinks Take It to the Net
pearsonsuccessnet.com | keyword: refraction
code: g4p422

Rays of light bend and separate into individual colors when they strike a piece of glass known as a prism. Red light bends the least. Violet light bends the most.

The Human Eye

The human eye is a fluid-filled ball with a bony area around it. A transparent covering protects the front of the eye. The covering also refracts light that enters the eye. A doughnut-shaped muscle called the iris is behind the covering. The iris is the colored part of the eye. The dark opening in the center of the iris is called the pupil.

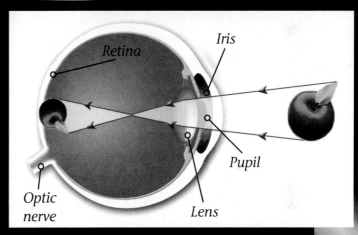

Retina

Iris

Pupil

Lens

Optic nerve

The iris controls how much light enters the eye. In bright light, the iris closes and the pupil gets smaller. In dim light, it opens and the pupil gets larger. The light that enters then passes through the lens of the eye. The lens refracts the light rays even more. The rays form an upside-down image on the retina at the back of the eye. Cells in the retina change the light into signals that travel along the optic nerve to the brain. You see a right-side up image.

1. ✓Checkpoint In which medium does light travel faster, a gas or a liquid?
2. Math in Science Suppose you are using a magnifying glass that makes objects seem 3 times their real-life size. How long would an insect that measures 1 centimeter look through the magnifying glass?

Lenses

Lenses are curved pieces of clear glass or plastic that refract light that passes through them. Lenses can be used to help people see things that are very small or very far away. There are two main types of lenses: convex and concave.

Convex Lenses

A convex lens is thicker in the middle than at the edges, somewhat like a football. When light passes through a convex lens, the light rays bend in toward the middle of the lens. The bent light rays come together and meet at a point on the other side of the lens. A convex lens can magnify things, or make them look larger. Magnifying glasses and microscopes contain convex lenses.

Concave Lenses

A concave lens is thinner in the middle than at the edges. When light passes through a concave lens, the light rays bend out toward the thicker edges of the lens. The light rays spread apart. So, the object appears smaller than it really is.

Concave lenses and convex lenses are often used together to make details look sharper. Many telescopes that are used to view distant objects have both concave and convex lenses.

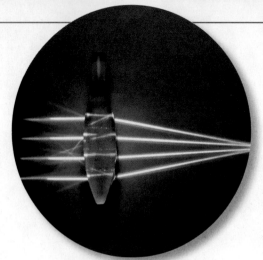

Convex lenses make things look larger.

Concave lenses make things look smaller.

1st century Roman thinker Seneca notices that a glass ball filled with water makes objects appear larger.

1275: On a visit to China, Italian traveler Marco Polo sees people wearing eyeglasses.

1609: Italian scientist Galileo uses a telescope to look at objects in the sky.

1668: English scientist Isaac Newton invents a new type of telescope with a reflecting mirror.

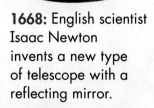

Ways Light Is Used

Lasers

A laser is a narrow but powerful beam of light. Laser light can be visible or invisible. It can travel long distances and still focus on a small area. You use laser light when you store information on or play a CD. Laser light is used to read bar codes in stores and libraries. It is used in printers and scanners.

Laser light has a great deal of heat energy. In industry, it is used to cut, drill, and bond materials together. In medicine, doctors use lasers to treat certain problems with internal organs, the eye, and the skin.

Optical Fibers

Optical fibers are very thin glass or plastic fibers that are bundled together in a coated, flexible tube. A light source, often a laser, is at one end of the tube. A human eye, a camera, or some other detector is at the other end. The tube can be twisted or bent without affecting the image that is sent.

Optical fibers are made from transparent materials that transmit visible, ultraviolet, and infrared light. The information they carry quickly travels long distances. Optical fibers are used in communication, medicine, and industry.

✔ Lesson Checkpoint

1. What happens to light energy when it is absorbed by an object?
2. What does a convex lens look like?
3. **Writing in Science** **Expository** Write a paragraph in your **science journal** that explains what happens when light rays strike a mirror.

1670s: Dutch scientist Anton van Leeuwenhoek becomes the first person to look at tiny life forms with a microscope.

1784: American Benjamin Franklin invents bifocal glasses, which help people see both near and far objects.

1800s: German scientist Joseph von Fraunhofer uses two different types of lenses to make a compound lens.

1888: Contact lenses are placed directly on the eye to correct eyesight.

Investigate How is light reflected and refracted?

Light travels in straight lines, but you can make it bend.

Materials

scissors

shoe box with hole

metric ruler and black paper

black paper square with slits

flashlight and mirror

cup and water

What to Do

1 Tape the black paper square over the hole in the box. Measure the bottom of the box. Cut black paper to fit.

2 Hold the flashlight about 60 cm from the box. Shine the light through the slits. See how the black paper absorbs most of the light, but some light goes through the slits. **Observe** the light's path inside the box.

60 cm

Your teacher will dim the lights.

3 Tilt a mirror in the box to reflect the light. Observe the light's path.

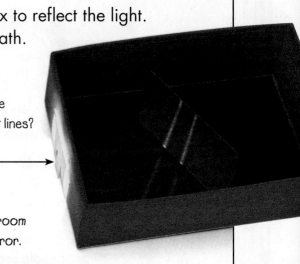

Do you see 2 straight lines?

60 cm

Find objects in your classroom that reflect light like a mirror.

④ Put an empty plastic cup in the box. Shine light through the slits and the cup. Observe how light passes through air in the cup. Add water. Observe how it refracts the light.

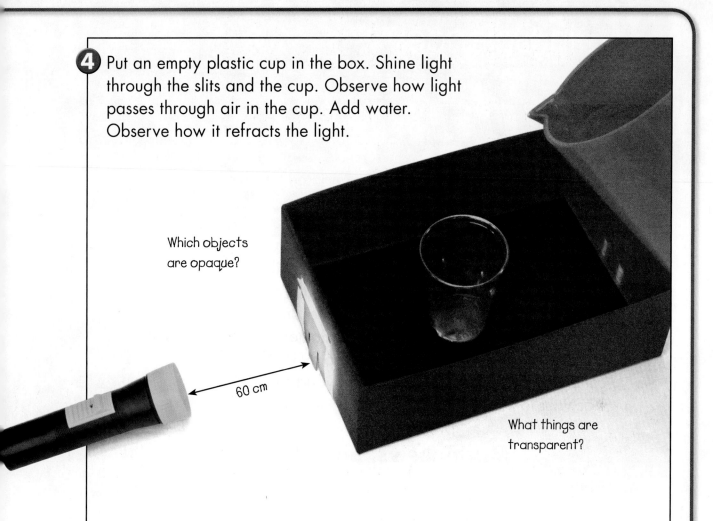

Which objects are opaque?

60 cm

What things are transparent?

⑤ Draw a sketch or diagram to show the path of the light from the flashlight, through the slits, through the water, and beyond.

Explain Your Results

1. Compare how light is affected by the air, the cup, the water, the box, the black paper, and the mirror. Use the terms *reflect, refract, absorb, opaque,* and *transparent.*

2. Describe the light's path through the box and the cup with water. **Infer** what happens when light travels from air to water.

Go Further

How is light affected by translucent materials, such as wax paper? Develop and carry out a written plan to answer this question or one of your own. When finished, give an oral report to your class or make a written report in your science journal.

427

Math in Science

Comparing Speeds

Sound travels through air at about 1,190 kilometers per hour. That means a sound can travel the length of a football field in about one third of a second. Many machines travel just as fast as sound. Some machines travel even faster than sound. The display below compares the speeds of some of the world's fastest machines to the speed of sound.

Machines vs. Sound

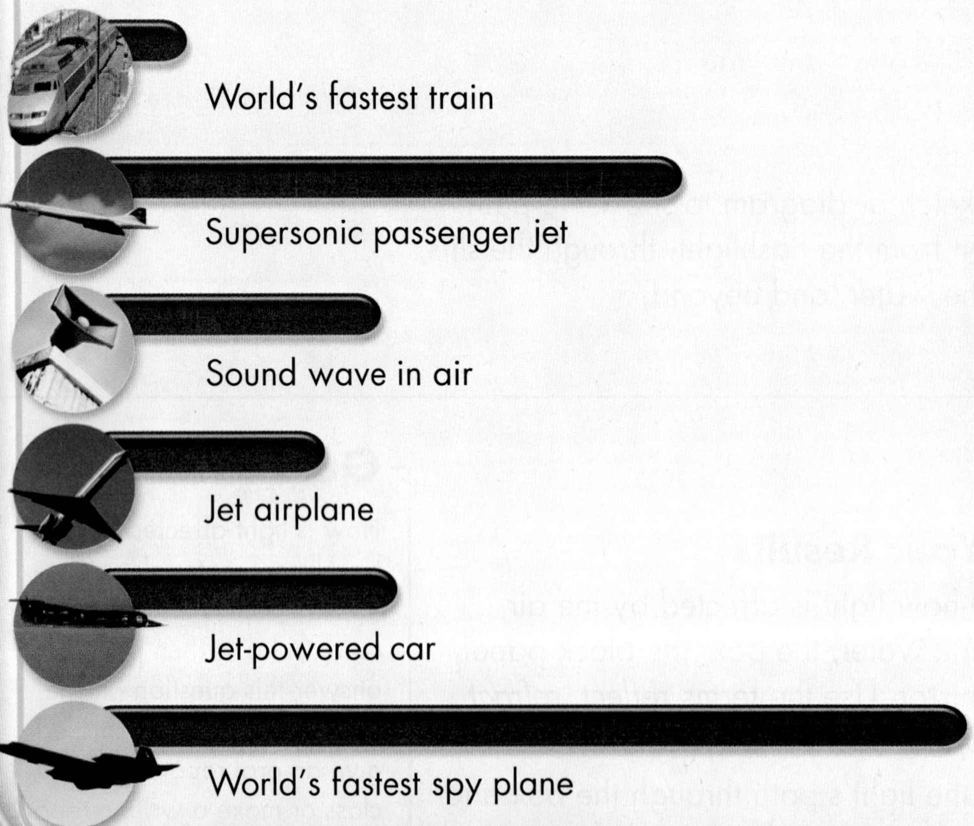
World's fastest train
Supersonic passenger jet
Sound wave in air
Jet airplane
Jet-powered car
World's fastest spy plane

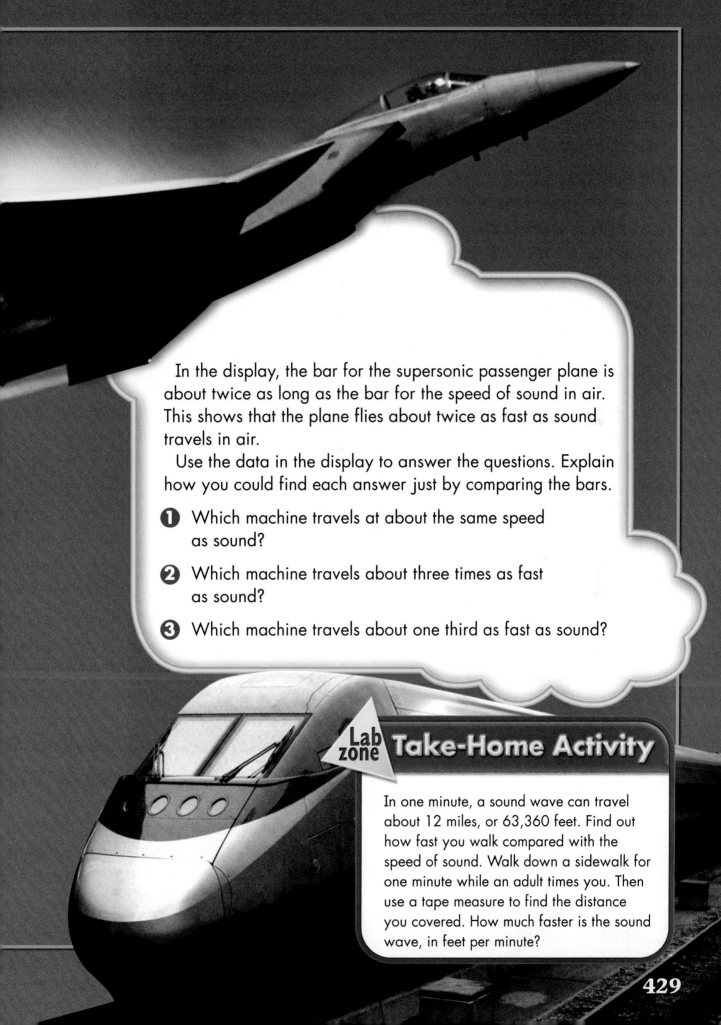

In the display, the bar for the supersonic passenger plane is about twice as long as the bar for the speed of sound in air. This shows that the plane flies about twice as fast as sound travels in air.

Use the data in the display to answer the questions. Explain how you could find each answer just by comparing the bars.

1 Which machine travels at about the same speed as sound?

2 Which machine travels about three times as fast as sound?

3 Which machine travels about one third as fast as sound?

Lab zone Take-Home Activity

In one minute, a sound wave can travel about 12 miles, or 63,360 feet. Find out how fast you walk compared with the speed of sound. Walk down a sidewalk for one minute while an adult times you. Then use a tape measure to find the distance you covered. How much faster is the sound wave, in feet per minute?

Chapter 14 Review and Test Prep

Use Vocabulary

absorption (p. 420)	**reflection** (p. 420)
compression (p. 408)	**refraction** (p. 422)
frequency (p. 409)	**translucent** (p. 421)
opaque (p. 421)	**transparent** (p. 421)
pitch (p. 412)	**wavelength** (p. 409)

Use the term from the list above that best completes each sentence.

1. Clear glass is an example of a(n) _____ material.

2. Light rays cannot pass through a material that is _____.

3. A sound wave with a high frequency will also have a high _____.

4. The distance from one point on a wave to the next similar point on a wave is known as _____.

5. _____ is bending that results from a light wave changing speed as it moves at an angle from one medium to another.

6. When a light wave is taken in by an object, _____ occurs.

7. Materials that let some light rays pass through but scatter some of the other rays are _____.

8. A wave bouncing back off an object or surface is known as _____.

9. A(n) _____ is the part of a sound wave where particles are close together.

10. The number of times a wave makes a complete cycle in a second is its _____.

Explain Concepts

11. Explain why a wave with a short wavelength has a high frequency.

12. Why does a light wave travel more slowly through a gas than through a vacuum?

Process Skills

13. **Predict** what a note played on a tuba would sound like if you were standing in front of the tuba player. Then predict what the note would sound like if the tuba player were at one end of a basketball court and you were standing at the other end.

14. Interpret the data The Sun gives off light energy in the visible and invisible parts of the electromagnetic spectrum. The circle graph shows the different kinds of light the Sun gives off. Explain whether most of the light energy given off is in the visible or the invisible part of the spectrum.

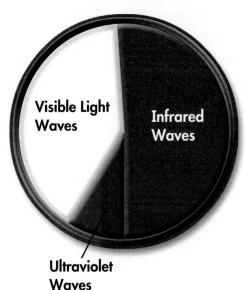

Visible Light Waves

Infrared Waves

Ultraviolet Waves

Draw Conclusions

15. Make a graphic organizer like the one shown below. Fill in facts that might lead you to the conclusion.

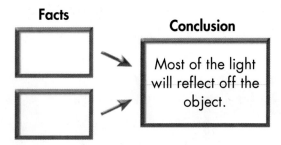

Facts

Conclusion

Most of the light will reflect off the object.

 Test Prep

Choose the letter that best completes the statement.

16. A sound wave cannot travel through a _____.
  Ⓐ gas   © solid
  Ⓑ liquid   Ⓓ vacuum

17. To hear a higher-pitched note on a guitar string you should
  Ⓕ loosen the string.
  Ⓖ shorten the string.
  Ⓗ pluck the string harder.
  Ⓘ make the string vibrate more slowly.

18. Radio waves, ultraviolet rays, and gamma rays are all
  Ⓐ part of the visible spectrum.
  Ⓑ part of the electromagnetic spectrum.
  © longitudinal waves.
  Ⓓ used to broadcast television and radio programs.

19. Explain why the answer you selected for Question 18 is best. For each answer you did not select, give a reason why it is not the best choice.

20. Writing in Science **Expository** Write a paragraph explaining what happens to a ray of sunlight as it passes from the air through a clear glass filled with water.

Optometrist

The eye is a sensitive organ and requires special care. Optometrists help us take care of our eyes. Sometimes people do not see everything clearly. They may see things that are close, but things that are far away seem blurry. They are nearsighted. Other people can see things far away but have a hard time seeing things up close. They are farsighted. An optometrist can prescribe lenses to correct these problems.

The kind of lens an optometrist prescribes depends on the kind of vision problem that needs to be corrected. The shape of the lens changes how light enters the eye.

Optometrists can help with other eye problems. They can diagnose and treat some eye diseases. They can check to see how well you see colors. They may recommend exercises to help your eyes work together better. Optometrists also can test your depth perception, the ability to judge how far away something is.

If you want to help people see better, you might like to become an optometrist. You must earn a college degree. The next step is to earn a Doctor of Optometry degree. You also must pass a test given by the state where you want to be an optometrist.

Lab zone Take-Home Activity

The way a camera works is similar to the way an eye works. Use a library or the Internet to find out how a camera works.

You Will Discover

- how types of motion are described.
- how forces affect motion.
- how forces, motion, and energy are related.

Chapter 15

Objects in Motion

online
Student Edition
pearsonsuccessnet.com

What causes motion and how does it affect us?

relative motion

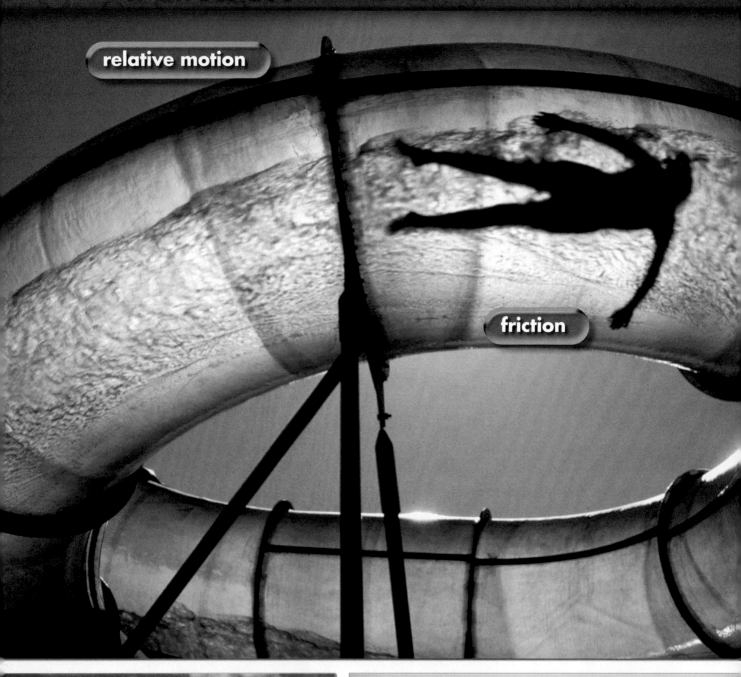

friction

velocity

force

work

434

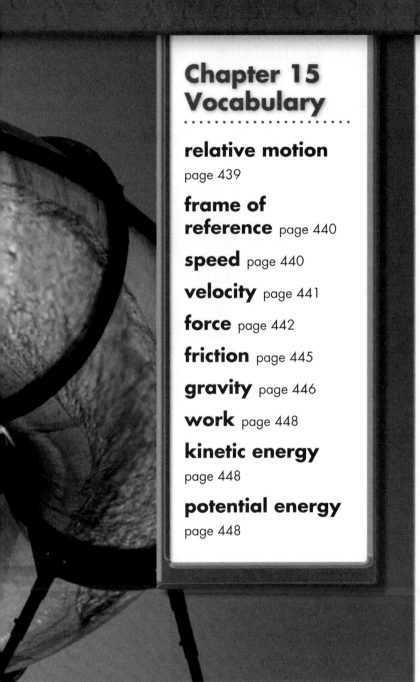

Chapter 15 Vocabulary

frame of reference

speed

gravity

kinetic energy

potential energy

Lab zone: Directed Inquiry

Explore What can change a marble's speed?

Materials

marble and ruler with groove

books and timer

meterstick and masking tape

calculator or computer (optional)

What to Do

1 Roll a marble down a ramp. Time how long it takes to move 180 cm. Find the speed.

speed = distance ÷ time

about 5 cm

Place marble at end of ruler.

book

ruler with a groove

Use masking tape to make a Starting Line and an Ending Line.

Starting Line

Begin timing here.

180 cm

Ending Line

Stop timing here.

2 Predict how raising the ramp would change the speed. Test your prediction by adding 1 book.

Explain Your Results

1. **Interpret Data** Make a bar graph to show your results.

2. **Infer** How did raising the ramp change the speed of the marble?

Reading Skills

Sequence

Sequence refers to the order in which events happen. Words such as *first, next, then, after,* and *finally* signal sequence. Knowing the order of events can help you **interpret data.**

Science Journal

Rolling Along

First, my friend gave me a ruler with a groove in the center. I put one end of the ruler on the floor and propped the other end on a book to form a ramp. Next, I put a marble in the groove at the high end of the ruler and let it go. When the marble stopped rolling, my friend used a piece of tape to mark how far it had traveled. I measured and recorded the distance the marble rolled on the floor. Then we did the same thing two more times. Finally we compared our results.

Apply It!

Use clue words to help you complete a graphic organizer that shows the order in which things happened in the journal entry.

Add as many boxes as you need to show the entire **sequence** of events.

First
⬇
| Next |
⬇
| Then |
⬇

◀))) You Are There!

You thought the stairs would never end, but finally you're at the top. You lower yourself into the steep, looping tube as water swirls around your feet. Then you let go. Suddenly, you're sliding, twisting, turning, faster and faster. At each curve, you fear that you'll fly right out of the tube, but your body slams against the wall and bounces back into the cushion of rushing water. After one last loop, you shoot out the end of the tube. Whoosh! You splash into the pool. You can't wait to go again, but you just don't know if you have the energy to climb all those stairs. If only you could slide up the stairs too! Why can't you?

◀ AudioText ◀))

Lesson 1

What is motion?

All kinds of things around you move in different ways. Cars, trucks, and buses transport people and goods from place to place. You can describe and measure their motion in different ways.

Types of Motion

Different things move in different ways. One way objects can move is in a straight line. A baseball player racing for home plate is likely to run in a straight line.

Sometimes toy cars move in a straight path on the track.

Sometimes the cars move in a curved path.

Objects can also move in a curved path. A car turning a corner moves in a curved path. Curved motion takes place around a center point. A spinning bicycle wheel follows a curved path around its axle. Earth moves in a curved path around the Sun.

Another way things can move is back and forth. When a player plucks a guitar string, the string moves back and forth. This back-and-forth motion is known as vibration.

As you ride your bicycle or walk down a street, though, you pass trees, buildings, and other things that do not move. They are fixed in place. When you pass a fixed object, you know you are moving. When you stand still, you can tell that a car you see moves if it changes position. Every day, you compare objects that change position with objects that don't. The change in one object's position compared with another object's position is **relative motion.**

1.   ✔ **Checkpoint** What are three different types of motion?
2.   ⟳ **Sequence** Describe the sequence of events of the yellow racecar as it travels around the track above.

From your frame of reference on the sidewalk, the bus and the people on it are moving.

From your frame of reference on the bus, everything on the bus seems to be standing still.

From your frame of reference on the bus, if the bus moves, everything outside it seems to move.

How You Know You Are Moving

How do you know if a person on a water slide moves? How do you know if the water moves? You look at the changing positions of the person and the water. You compare their changing positions with the fixed position of the slide. You use the relative motion of the objects around you to decide what is moving and what is not moving.

Objects that don't seem to move define your **frame of reference.** How an object seems to move depends on your frame of reference. Your frame of reference is like your point of view.

Suppose you are on a float in a parade. Your friend is on the same float. The float begins moving down the parade route. You wave at the people sitting and watching the parade as your float moves past them. From your frame of reference on the float, the people seem to be moving. But, your friend hasn't moved a bit. From your friend's frame of reference, you haven't moved either. As the parade moves down the street, people on the sidewalk see you and your friend pass by. From their frame of reference, you and your friend are both moving.

Suppose you use your classroom as your frame of reference. If you were sitting at your desk, you would say that you are not moving. But suppose you choose the Sun as your frame of reference. Now you would say that you are moving, because Earth carries you along with it as it travels around the Sun.

Measuring Motion

Speed is the rate at which an object changes position. It measures how fast an object moves. The unit for speed is a unit of distance divided by a unit of time, such as kilometers per hour. A car moving at a high speed changes position faster than a car moving at a slow speed. To find an object's average speed, divide the distance the object moves by the total time spent moving.

Velocity combines both the speed and the direction an object is moving. Some words that describe direction are *north*, *south*, *east*, and *west*. Others are *left*, *right*, *up*, and *down*.

Any change in the speed or direction of an object's motion is an acceleration. Starting, speeding up, and slowing down are accelerations. The roller coaster accelerates as it speeds up. It is changing speed. A roller coaster on a curved path accelerates even if its speed does not change. That is because it changes direction as it moves around the curve.

✓ **Lesson Checkpoint**

1. What is a frame of reference?
2. What are two ways that a roller coaster can accelerate?
3. Writing in Science **Descriptive** Write a paragraph in your **science journal** that describes the difference between speed and velocity.

The roller coaster slows as it moves up to the top of the loop. It goes faster heading downhill. The velocity changes as the coaster changes direction from up to down.

As the roller coaster moves uphill again, its velocity changes. Its speed decreases.

This roller coaster reaches its greatest speed at the bottom of the loop.

441

How does force affect moving objects?

Objects do not just move on their own. Something must make a ball start to roll. Something must also make a rolling ball stop.

Force

A **force** is any push or pull. Force can make an object that is standing still start to move. It can also make a moving object move faster, slow down, stop, or change direction. The object moves in the same direction as the force.

Some forces act only on contact. These forces must touch an object to affect it. A marble on a level surface will not move until you hit it with your finger or another object. Contact force starts the ball rolling.

Other forces can act at a distance. These forces can affect objects without touching them. For example, without any contact, a magnet can pull a piece of iron toward it. The magnet has a force that acts on the iron from a distance.

Pushing or pulling can change both the position and motion of an object. The size of the change depends on the strength of the push or pull. For example, the harder you push a swing, the higher and faster it will move. Also, a strong magnet will pull a piece of iron toward it from farther away than a weak magnet will.

A moving marble hits one that is standing still. The contact force of the moving marble starts the other marble moving.

A marble that is standing still moves when it is bumped by another marble.

Magnets can make things move without touching them.

Magnetism is a force that can act at a distance. Magnetic force has an effect on metals such as iron and steel.

442

Combining Forces

All forces have both size and direction. Notice the dogs pulling on the rubber toy. They are combining forces, but they are working against each other. They are pulling in opposite directions, but with the same amount of force. As long as they both pull with forces that are the same size, the forces are balanced. The toy will not move. But if one dog pulls with more force, the forces will be unbalanced. The toy will move toward the dog with the greater force.

Many objects are acted upon by more than one force. Suppose you push on a door to open it. Your friend on the other side of the door also pushes on it with the same size force. But your friend is pushing the door in the opposite direction. The forces are balanced and the door does not move. But suppose you continue to push the door while your friend pulls it. Now both forces are acting on the door in the same direction. The door moves—quickly—in your friend's direction. The total force on the door can be found by adding the forces together.

Two train engines pull together in the same direction. They are combining forces and working together. The total force of the engines is equal to the sum of the two forces.

1. ✔ **Checkpoint** What causes objects to move or moving objects to stop moving?
2. ➌ **Sequence** Describe the sequence of events if the dog on the right suddenly stops pulling on the toy.

Force and Motion

If two dogs tug on a toy with balanced force, the toy will not move. Balanced forces acting in opposite directions cancel each other. The object's motion does not change. A still object cannot start moving unless the forces acting on it change. The resistance an object has to any change to its motion is called inertia.

In the same way, a moving object changes its motion only when a force acts on it. If balanced forces are applied to a moving object, it will keep moving at the same speed and in the same direction. The moving object will not slow, speed up, or turn until the forces acting on it become unbalanced.

The amount of force acting on an object affects how that object changes speed and direction. When you ride a bike, you push the pedals. If you push harder, the bicycle goes faster. You turn the handlebars. The bicycle changes direction.

More force is needed to change the motion of an object with more mass. That's why you can easily move an empty wagon. When your friends climb in, you must pull with more force to move the wagon and its passengers.

Force is needed to move the plow. Even more force would be needed to move larger equipment.

Friction

You learned that a moving object will not slow until the forces acting on it change. You also know that if you don't pull a wagon, it will eventually slow and stop. Actually, the wagon slows because there is a force acting on it.

Friction is a force that acts when two surfaces rub together. Friction can slow or stop moving objects. It can also keep objects from starting to move. The amount of friction between two surfaces depends on each object's surface and on how hard the objects press together.

Changing Friction

The surface of every object has high and low spots. When rough surfaces rub, the high spots catch on each other, causing a lot of friction. On a smooth surface, the uneven places are too tiny to see or feel. When smooth surfaces rub, there is less friction. The objects move more easily.

The amount of friction also depends on how hard the objects press together. If you push a box of feathers along the floor, it moves easily. What would happen if you fill the same box with books instead? The box of books presses against the floor with more force. This greater force causes more friction, so the box of books is harder to push.

If you can't change the objects' surfaces or how hard they press together, you can reduce friction in other ways. You can use oil or wax to make the surfaces smoother. Less friction means you need less force to move the objects.

The surface of the Super Slide is very smooth.

Ball bearings reduce friction because they roll rather than drag across each other. Oil makes their surfaces smoother.

✓ **Lesson Checkpoint**

1. What is friction?
2. **Writing in Science** **Descriptive** Write a short story in your **science journal** describing what would happen if suddenly there was no friction.

445

Mass and Weight

Mass and weight are not the same. Mass is the amount of matter in an object. Weight is a measure of the force of gravity acting on that object's mass. The Moon's mass is much less than Earth's mass. So the Moon pulls things toward it with only one-sixth as much force. This means that people on the Moon weigh only one-sixth as much as they do on Earth. But their mass does not change.

Lesson 3

How are force, mass, and energy related?

The force of gravity acts between all objects. How gravity and other forces act depends on the mass, distance, and motion of the objects.

The heavier the weight is, the more it stretches the spring.

The Force of Gravity

When you drop a ball, it doesn't hang in the air. Instead, it falls to the ground. A force acts on the ball to make it fall. That force is **gravity**, which makes objects pull toward each other. The force of gravity between two objects depends on their masses and the distance between them.

The force of gravity is stronger if objects are close together. As the objects move farther apart, the force of gravity between them becomes weaker.

The force of gravity between massive objects is strong. As the mass of the objects is reduced, so is the force of gravity between them. Doubling the mass of one object doubles the force of gravity between it and another object.

The ball you drop falls because Earth's large mass pulls on it. The ball also pulls on Earth, but the ball's mass is too small to move a mass as large as Earth.

The astronaut weighs about 900 newtons on Earth but only about 150 newtons on the Moon.

446

Sir Isaac Newton made many discoveries that relate force and motion.

Measuring Force

The amount and direction of many forces can be measured. A spring scale is one tool used to measure force. A spring scale has a hook on the bottom. An object hanging from the hook stretches the spring inside. How much the spring stretches depends on the object's weight. Weight is a measure of the force of gravity acting on an object's mass. The heavier an object is, the stronger the force. And the stronger the force, the more the spring will stretch. Look at the springs in the picture at the top of page 446. The heaviest weight stretched the spring the most.

The marker on the spring scale shows the size of the force that has stretched the spring. As the spring stretches, the marker moves along a row of numbers on the scale. These numbers are the unit of force that scientists call the newton. One newton (1 N) is about the force you would need to lift a small apple. The newton was named after Sir Isaac Newton, who explained how force and motion are linked.

1.   ✔Checkpoint) What two factors affect the force of gravity between two objects?
2.   Math in Science) If a dog weighed about 240 newtons on Earth, how much would it weigh on the Moon?

The wrecking ball has a great deal of kinetic energy before it crashes into the building.

Energy and Motion

Scientists define energy as the ability to do work. **Work** is the ability to move something. When work is done, a change happens. Energy is the source of that change. Any change in motion requires energy.

You should know about two kinds of energy. The energy of motion is **kinetic energy.** All moving things have kinetic energy. The amount of kinetic energy depends on an object's speed and mass. The faster the giant swing in the photo moves, the more kinetic energy it has. The swing also has more kinetic energy if the cage is full of riders. That is because the added mass of the riders has increased the total mass of the cage.

Stored Energy

When the swing reaches the top of its path, it stops for a moment. The swing is not moving, so it has no kinetic energy. But now it has another kind of energy. **Potential energy** is stored energy. The swing has potential energy because of its position at the top of its path. The swing has the most potential energy when it is as high as it can possibly be. As soon as the cage starts to swing down toward the ground, it starts to use its potential energy. Now that the cage is moving, the stored energy is changing to energy of motion.

Objects that are stretched or squeezed also have potential energy. A stretched rubber band has potential energy. So does the tightened spring in a wind-up toy.

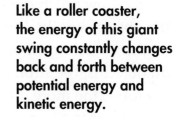

Like a roller coaster, the energy of this giant swing constantly changes back and forth between potential energy and kinetic energy.

Changing Energy

Potential energy can change into kinetic energy and back again. Picture a child winding the spring of the toy bird. Each turn adds more stored energy. Then the child releases the toy. The spring unwinds, and the bird hops forward. The energy stored in the spring is changing into the energy of motion.

At the top of its path, the giant swing has potential energy. As it swoops toward the ground, its stored energy changes to kinetic energy. When it swings back up to the top of its path, the energy of motion again becomes the stored energy of position. The giant swing starts back down, and the process starts again.

The wound spring inside this toy has potential energy.

In the giant swing, you saw that energy can change from one type to another. By nudging a rock so that it starts rolling down a hill, you change the rock's potential energy into kinetic energy. The potential energy that fuel gives a car changes to kinetic energy when the car drives forward. Energy cannot be made or destroyed. The total amount of energy never changes.

Changing Energy		
Type of Stored Energy	**How the Energy Is Used**	
Fossil fuels store potential energy from the Sun.	Fossil fuels burn to give cars and other vehicles kinetic energy.	
Plants store potential energy from the Sun.	The energy is released to support the animals that eat the plants.	
The water behind a dam has potential energy.	A hydroelectric power plant produces electric energy.	

✓ **Lesson Checkpoint**

1. What kind of energy does a stretched rubber band have?
2. How is energy changed in the toy bird?
3. **Technology** in Science Use the Internet or other sources to find out how Niagara Falls became a source of electrical energy.

Lab zone Guided Inquiry

Investigate How does friction affect motion?

Materials

Pattern for a
Ramp Angle Protractor

cardboard

sandpaper and
waxed paper

tape

toy car and eraser

calculator or computer
(optional)

Process Skills

You can use a table or a chart to **collect** and record **data**.

What to Do

1 Tape the sandpaper to the cardboard.

2 Put the car and the eraser on the ramp at the top. Have someone in your group hold the Ramp Angle Protractor.

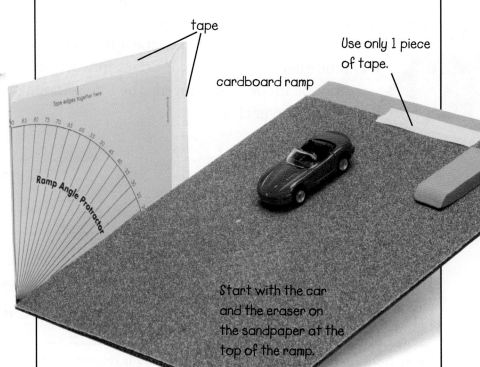

tape

cardboard ramp

Use only 1 piece of tape.

Ramp Angle Protractor

Start with the car and the eraser on the sandpaper at the top of the ramp.

3 Use your hand to slowly raise the ramp. **Observe** the angle of the ramp. When each object reaches the bottom of the ramp, record the angle. Repeat 2 more times. **Collect** and record your **data**.

4 Based on your observations, **predict** what would happen if you replaced the sandpaper with waxed paper. Test your prediction 3 times. Record your data.

5 Make a bar graph of your results.

	Angle at Which Object Reached Bottom of Ramp (degrees)			
	Sandpaper Surface		Waxed-Paper Surface	
	Car	Eraser	Car	Eraser
Trial 1				
Trial 2				
Trial 3				
Average				

Find the averages. Your teacher might ask you to use a calculator or a computer to find the averages.

Sandpaper is rougher than waxed paper. Compare the force of friction of the 2 surfaces.

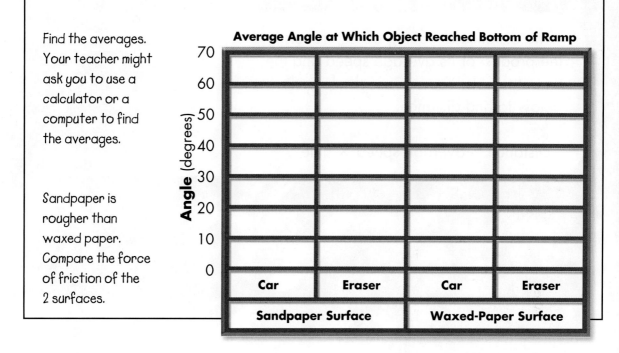

Average Angle at Which Object Reached Bottom of Ramp

Angle (degrees): 70, 60, 50, 40, 30, 20, 10, 0

Car | Eraser | Car | Eraser
Sandpaper Surface | Waxed-Paper Surface

Explain Your Results

1. **Interpreting Data** How did using waxed paper instead of sandpaper affect the angle at which the objects moved?

2. What force pulled the eraser down the ramp? What force kept the eraser from moving until the ramp was steep enough?

Go Further

How could you increase or decrease the force of friction between the objects and the ramp? Design and conduct a scientific investigation to find out. Provide evidence for your conclusion.

Relating Distance, Speed, and Time

The distance a moving object travels is the product of its average speed and the time it travels. You can use the formula below to find distance.

Distance = average speed × time

In the 1850s, wagons on the Oregon Trail traveled at an average speed of 3 km per hour. At this pace, they could travel only 3 × 8 km, or 24 km, in 8 hours. Today, at highway speeds, you can travel 24 kilometers in a car in 15 minutes or less.

Use the distance formula to answer each question.

1 Today, a car traveling on a highway might have an average speed of 92 kilometers per hour. How far would the car travel in 8 hours?

2 A jet passenger plane might have an average speed of 775 kilometers per hour. If an international flight takes 8 hours, how far has the plane traveled?

3 A roller coaster travels an 852-meter track in 3 minutes. What is the average speed of the roller coaster in meters per minute?

Lab zone Take-Home Activity

Plan a trip with the following conditions. You have 4 hours to travel each way. You may go by car, train, or airplane. Choose a destination you could reach from home by your choice of transportation in 4 hours.

Chapter 15 Review and Test Prep

Use Vocabulary

force (p. 442)	**potential energy** (p. 448)
frame of reference (p. 440)	**relative motion** (p. 439)
friction (p. 445)	**speed** (p. 440)
gravity (p. 446)	**velocity** (p. 441)
kinetic energy (p. 448)	**work** (p. 448)

Use the vocabulary term from the list above that best completes each sentence.

1. A child at the top of a slide has _____.

2. When you push or pull on a wagon, you make a _____ act on the wagon.

3. _____ tells both the speed and direction that something is moving.

4. _____ is done when you move an object.

5. A change in the position of one object compared with the position of another object is called _____.

6. The force that makes a ball fall toward the ground is _____.

7. Objects that don't seem to move define your _____.

8. The energy that a bicycle has when it moves is called _____.

Explain Concepts

9. Why do you need to use force to move a ball up a ramp when it moves downward by itself?

10. Use vocabulary terms to explain why a soccer ball that is quickly rolling across a grass field slows and finally stops rolling.

Process Skills

11. **Infer** Why is it easier to push an empty grocery cart than one that is filled with canned foods?

12. **Predict** what would happen if you tried to walk on a sidewalk where there was no friction between your shoes and the sidewalk.

13. Classify Copy the chart below. Then classify each motion as straight line, curved, or vibration.

Motion	Kind of Motion
Swinging back and forth on a swing	
Riding on a merry-go-round	
Crossing the street at a crosswalk	

 **Sequence**

14. Complete a graphic organizer to show the order in which things happen on a roller coaster ride.

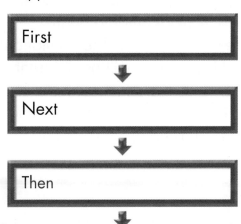

First

↓

Next

↓

Then

↓

 Test Prep

Choose the letter that best completes the statement or answers the question.

15. Gravity is a force that makes objects
  Ⓐ push apart.
  Ⓑ pull toward each other.
  Ⓒ stop moving.
  Ⓓ move uphill.

16. Which object has kinetic energy?
  Ⓕ a ball lying on the floor
  Ⓖ a stopped merry-go-round
  Ⓗ a dog running through a yard
  Ⓘ a car parked in a garage

17. What happens to the force of gravity between two objects when the mass of one of the objects is increased?
  Ⓐ It increases.
  Ⓑ It decreases.
  Ⓒ It stays the same.
  Ⓓ It pushes the objects apart.

18. Speed is expressed in units of
  Ⓕ time per distance.
  Ⓖ direction per time.
  Ⓗ distance per time.
  Ⓘ force per time.

19. Explain why the answer you selected for Question 16 is best. For each answer you did not select, give a reason why it is not the best choice.

20. Writing in Science **Descriptive**
Write a paragraph describing what types of motion take place during a tug-of-war.

455

Career

Space Engineer

Estela Hernandez is a flight simulation engineer for NASA.

Would you like to be part of the space program when you grow up? Even if flying in space is not something you would like to do, you can still work for NASA.

Most space engineers do not go into space. Their work is here on Earth. An engineer at NASA might work on many different projects. Engineers design the Space Shuttle, the computers, and everything that the space vehicle needs to reach its destination, complete its tasks, and return home safely. Engineers design such things as the places where the astronauts will live or the Space Shuttle lands.

Engineers also design simulations on Earth. A simulation is a model of an actual event that helps us learn about the real thing. Simulations of gravity in space or of flying in a Space Shuttle help engineers design the Space Shuttle. Simulations also help astronauts learn what to do in different situations when they are in space. The simulations prepare astronauts for how life in space will be different from life on Earth.

Math skills are used often in engineering. If engineering interests you, you will want to start now. Study all the math and science you can.

Lab zone Take-Home Activity

Think of something you would like to improve. Maybe you want skates with better brakes or a clock that tells what the weather is like. Write about your idea.

456

You Will Discover

- how simple machines help us do work.
- how simple machines work together as parts of complex machines.

Chapter 16

Simple Machines

Web Games
Take It to the Net
pearsonsuccessnet.com

online
Student Edition
pearsonsuccessnet.com

64mm

How do simple machines make work easier?

fulcrum

effort

lever

pulley

inclined plane

load

458

Chapter 16 Vocabulary

wheel and axle

wedge

screw

459

Explore How can a machine ring a bell?

Materials

2 markers

2 metric rulers

eraser

marble

bell

What to Do

1 Set up a machine that can ring a bell. Your machine could look like the one in the picture.

Push down.

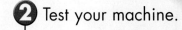

2 Test your machine.

Process Skills

You can **communicate** information about the machine you made by drawing a diagram.

Explain Your Results

1. Draw a diagram that **communicates** how to make the machine. Draw another diagram that communicates how the machine works.

2. How else could you use the machine? What else could you make with the parts?

Reading Skills

TARGET SKILL

Summarize

A **summary** is a short retelling of something you have read. You can use a summary to **communicate** the most important ideas.

• Leave out most details, and do not add any new ideas.

• Use your own words when you summarize.

• A graphic organizer can help you organize the information for your summary.

Science Article

Musical Levers

Many musical instruments use levers to play different notes. A piano key is connected to levers inside the piano. The levers move a hammer that hits a group of strings that make the sounds. Flutes and clarinets have levers that open and close small holes. Opening and closing different holes make different sounds. Drummers use levers attached to hammers that strike the drums.

Apply It!

Read the science article. Use a graphic organizer to choose which ideas you want to **communicate.** Then write a one- or two-sentence **summary** about "Musical Levers."

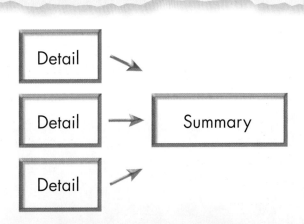

Detail →

Detail → Summary

Detail →

You Are There!

On the way home from school, you walk by an empty lot. You see a huge machine digging a hole. A shovel on the end of a long arm scoops up dirt. It dumps the dirt into a dump truck. You watch carefully for a while, thinking about how the parts of the machine work together. Some parts look familiar. How do small, simple machines work together to do big jobs?

AudioText

Lesson 1
What is a machine?

A lever is a simple machine. It helps people do work. Other simple machines include the wheel and axle, pulley, inclined plane, wedge, and screw.

Work

Do you think that work means doing homework or chores? In science, work has a special meaning. Work means using force—pushing or pulling—to move an object or make a change.

You could use a lot of force but not do any work. Suppose you push as hard as you can on a brick wall. You may push very hard, but you won't move the wall. Because nothing moves or changes, you aren't doing any work.

Machines Make Work Easier

A machine can be just one piece or it can have many parts. However, all machines help us do work. Some simple machines allow you to use less force to do work. The heavier the object, the more force you must use to move it. Without simple machines, we couldn't budge heavy things.

Other simple machines change the direction of force. You can push or pull in one direction and get work done in a different direction.

You will learn about simple machines that have just one or two parts. Yet each machine makes work easier. Some basic types of simple machines are the lever, the pulley, the inclined plane, the wheel and axle, the wedge, and the screw.

1.   ✓ **Checkpoint** How do you use force to do work?
2.   **Writing in Science** **Descriptive** Distance is the amount of space between two things. In your **science journal,** write a paragraph that describes how you would measure the distance someone pushes a wheelbarrow. Be sure your description includes the tools and the units you would use.

Levers

One useful machine is the lever. A **lever** is a long bar with a support. The weight of both the bar and what it carries rests on the support. We call this support the **fulcrum.** The object you want to move is the **load.** When you use a lever, you have to apply some effort, or force. The **effort** is a push or a pull on the bar that makes the load move in some way.

A lever doesn't make you stronger, but it does make doing hard work easier. It adds to your force. It can also change the direction of the force.

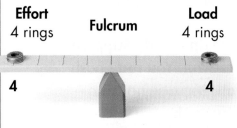

Effort		Load
4 rings	**Fulcrum**	4 rings

4   4

The effort and the load are equal. Each is 4 units from the fulcrum.

Effort		Load
4 rings	**Fulcrum**	8 rings

4   2

On this lever, the effort is 4 units from the fulcrum, but the load is only 2 units from it. The same effort balances a larger load.

Using a Lever

The first picture shows a lever with the fulcrum exactly halfway between the load and the effort. The effort you use matches the downward force of the load. The lever changes the direction of the force. You push down on the effort side to lift the load up.

In the second picture, the fulcrum is closer to the load than to the effort. The load, on the right, is a stack of eight rings. The effort, on the left, is a stack of four rings. When the fulcrum of a lever is closer to the load, the effort is applied over a greater distance. You use the same effort to lift a heavier object.

For any lever, the effort times its distance from the fulcrum is equal to the load times its distance from the fulcrum. This equation matches the second picture.

Effort	×	**Distance**	=	**Load**	×	**Distance**
4	×	4	=	8	×	2
	16		=		16	

Levers help us lift things that are very heavy.

464

Types of Levers

Levers can be classified into three different groups. In the first group of levers, the fulcrum is between the effort and the load. Levers with the load between the effort and the fulcrum are in the second group. When the effort is between the load and the fulcrum, the lever is in the third group.

Groups of Levers

Some levers have two bars that work together. Levers with two bars can also be divided into groups.

Group 1

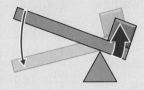

The fulcrum on the pliers is between the effort and the load. The effort is the part of the pliers you squeeze, and the load is the object you want to hold or turn.

Group 2

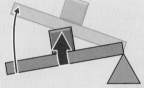

The fulcrum on the nutcracker is at the closed end. The effort is at the open end, where you squeeze. The load is the nut you want to crack open. It is between the fulcrum and the effort.

Group 3

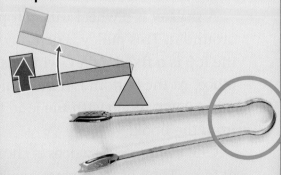

The fulcrum on the tongs is at the closed end. The load is at the open end, which picks up the ice cube. The effort is in the middle, where you squeeze. It is between the fulcrum and the load.

1. ✓**Checkpoint** Define fulcrum, load, and effort.
2. **Math in Science** A load of 3 rings is 4 units from the fulcrum of a lever. When 2 rings are placed on the other side of the fulcrum, the lever balances. How far are the 2 rings from the fulcrum?

Wheel and Axle

The **wheel and axle** is a special kind of lever that moves or turns objects. The axle is a rod that goes through the center of the wheel. A screwdriver is a good example of a wheel and axle. The handle is the wheel, and the metal blade is the axle. The end of the blade fits into a slot on the screw. You use force to turn the handle. The blade turns and tightens the screw.

Screwdriver

The door knob is another type of wheel and axle. You use force to turn the knob, or wheel. This force changes into a larger force that turns the axle. The axle is the turning shaft inside the doorknob.

Doorknob

Look at the picture of the garden hose reel. You turn the crank, and the long hose winds onto the reel. The crank you turn is the wheel. It is joined to the axle, which goes through the center of the reel. You use effort to turn the crank. With each turn, more hose is wound up!

Garden hose reel

Pulley

A **pulley** is a wheel with a rope, wire, or chain around it. This pulley is actually two pulleys. At the top is a fixed pulley, which is fastened to one place. At the bottom is a movable pulley. It moves up or down along with the load that is hanging from the hook.

One thing a pulley does is change the direction of force. Look at the picture again. The force scale shows how much force is being used to raise the weight. The strong pull from down and to the right makes the load go up. The pulley has changed the direction of the force.

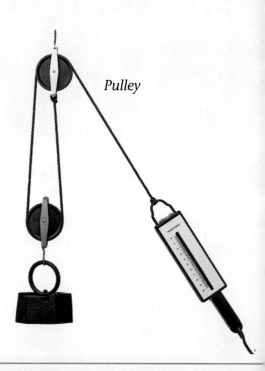
Pulley

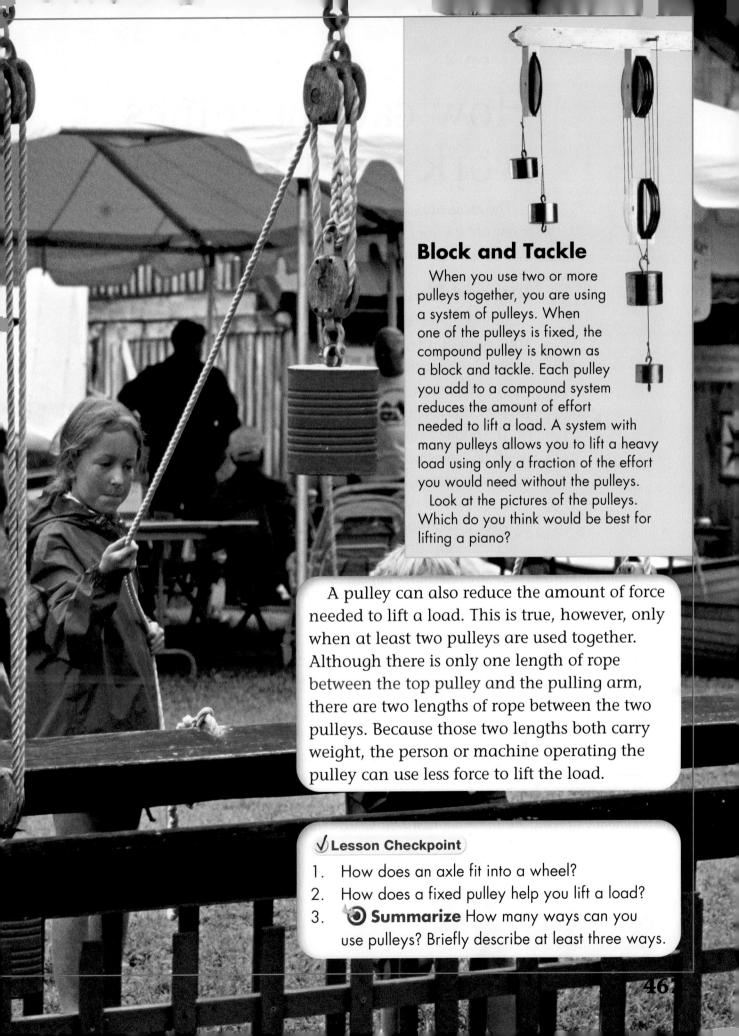

Block and Tackle

When you use two or more pulleys together, you are using a system of pulleys. When one of the pulleys is fixed, the compound pulley is known as a block and tackle. Each pulley you add to a compound system reduces the amount of effort needed to lift a load. A system with many pulleys allows you to lift a heavy load using only a fraction of the effort you would need without the pulleys.

Look at the pictures of the pulleys. Which do you think would be best for lifting a piano?

A pulley can also reduce the amount of force needed to lift a load. This is true, however, only when at least two pulleys are used together. Although there is only one length of rope between the top pulley and the pulling arm, there are two lengths of rope between the two pulleys. Because those two lengths both carry weight, the person or machine operating the pulley can use less force to lift the load.

✓ Lesson Checkpoint

1. How does an axle fit into a wheel?
2. How does a fixed pulley help you lift a load?
3. **⊙ Summarize** How many ways can you use pulleys? Briefly describe at least three ways.

467

Lesson 2

How can machines work together?

The inclined plane is a simple machine. The wedge and the screw are special kinds of inclined planes. Simple machines can be connected to do all kinds of work.

Inclined Plane

Suppose you want to put a heavy box of books on your desk. You could lift the box from the floor straight to your desk— ouch! Can you think of an easier way?

Did you think of making a ramp? If you could find a long, strong board, you could place one end on the floor and one end on the edge of the desk. Then you could push the heavy box up the flat, smooth surface of the ramp (the board). That would be a lot easier than lifting the box straight up!

In science, a ramp is a simple machine called an **inclined plane.** You do the same amount of work when you lift an object straight up as when you slide it up to the same level on an inclined plane. On an inclined plane, you use less force over a greater distance. You may think the job is easier, but you did the same work.

Factors That Affect Force

Inclined planes can help move objects up or down. Several factors affect the amount of force needed to move an object. If two ramps are the same height but different lengths, a greater force is needed to move an object up the shorter, steeper ramp. Suppose two boxes are at the bottom of an inclined plane. One box is very heavy. The other is light. Which box would you have to push harder to get to the top? That's right, the heavy box. You use more force to move heavier things.

Less force is needed to move up inclined planes that aren't very steep.

More force is needed to move up a steep inclined plane.

Suppose you and a friend race to push heavy boxes to the top of an inclined plane. Who used more force? Whoever took less time used more force. The stronger a force is, the faster it will move an object.

Friction can slow things as they move along an inclined plane. Friction is a force that develops between surfaces that rub. Friction makes pushing, dragging, or sliding things harder.

A box near the top of an inclined plane often stays where it is because the force of friction balances the downward-pulling force of gravity.

However, if you attach wheels to the bottom of the box, it will probably roll down the inclined plane. The wheels reduce most of the friction. The forces are unbalanced. Now gravity has greater force than friction.

1. ✓ **Checkpoint** You move a heavy box up an inclined plane, farther than if you lifted it straight up to the same height. Is using the inclined plane a good idea? Explain your answer.

2. **Social Studies** in Science Many roads in mountainous areas are built as zigzag inclined planes called switchbacks. What effect do the switchbacks have on the effort travelers use and the distance they travel?

469

Wedges

A **wedge** is a special kind of inclined plane. Wedges can be used to split things apart or to move things. They can also be used to hold things in place.

To do its work of splitting things apart, the wedge must be moving. A force aimed against the end of the wedge drives the inclined planes forward. The force can drive the thin edge of the wedge deep into an object.

In the picture below, you can see a wedge being driven into part of an old tree trunk. The force of the hammer pounding on the flat end of the wedge drives the pointed end of the wedge deeper and deeper into the wood. The wedge changes the downward force of the hammer into a sideways force that will split the wood into smaller pieces.

A nail is a kind of wedge. You drive a nail into wood by striking the flat end of the nail with a hammer. The nail fastens the wood to something else.

A force at the thick end of the wedge pushes the narrow end into the log.

A wedge used as a wheel block stops much larger objects from moving.

Screws That Drill Holes

An auger is a type of screw. It is used to drill holes. The auger twists downward. At the same time, pieces of the material being drilled move upward.

The people in the photo are drilling a hole in the ice sheet in Antarctica. They will study the ice that the auger brings from deep in the hole to the surface.

Screws

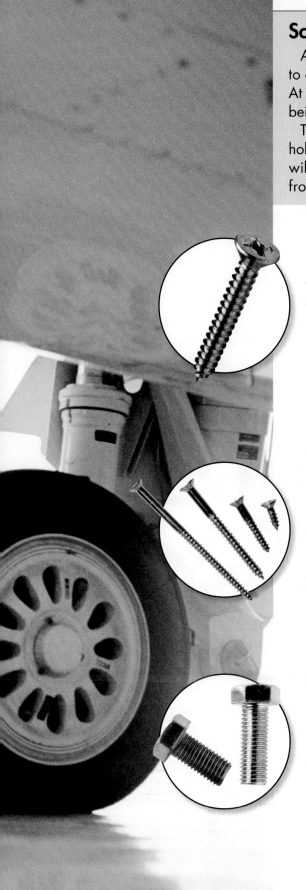

Another simple machine is the **screw.** Perhaps you have seen someone using a screwdriver to tighten a screw. Did you look closely at the screw? It is like a small stick with slanting ridges wrapped around it. We call these ridges *threads* of the screw.

Actually, the screw is a type of inclined plane. If you could unwrap a screw's threads, you would clearly see the inclined plane. The pictures at the right will help you see how this might look.

Screws are used in many ways. They can lift things. They can also fasten things. To tighten a screw, you must make many turns with a screwdriver. But a screw holds pieces of wood together better than a nail does because the threads make it hard to pull out the screw.

1. **✓Checkpoint** What part does an inclined plane play in a wedge? in a screw?

2. **Writing in Science** **Persuasive** Suppose you have made an auger for a special purpose. Write an advertisement to persuade people to buy it. Be sure to explain the special type of work the auger is designed to do.

471

Complex Machines

Simple machines are often put together to do bigger jobs. Complex machines have parts that are simple machines working together. *Complex* means "having many parts."

At home, you probably have a can opener in your kitchen. Does it look like the one below? Which simple machines are parts of the can opener? You can see circle shapes, so there are probably wheels and axles. Some of the wheels have spikes or points. They are *gears.* The spikes are called *teeth.* A gear is a kind of wheel. Gears are often used in pairs to change the speed or direction of motion.

Look carefully at the garden shears. Levers combined with wedges on the cutting blades make this a complex machine.

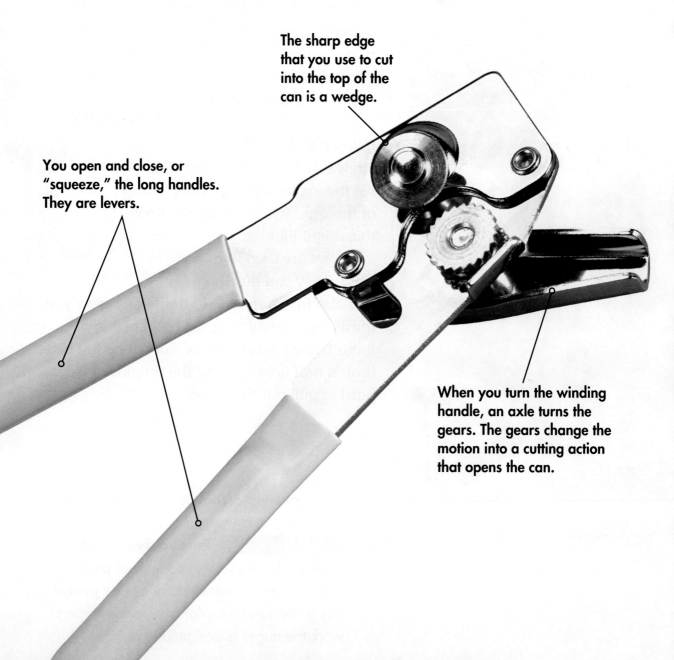

The sharp edge that you use to cut into the top of the can is a wedge.

You open and close, or "squeeze," the long handles. They are levers.

When you turn the winding handle, an axle turns the gears. The gears change the motion into a cutting action that opens the can.

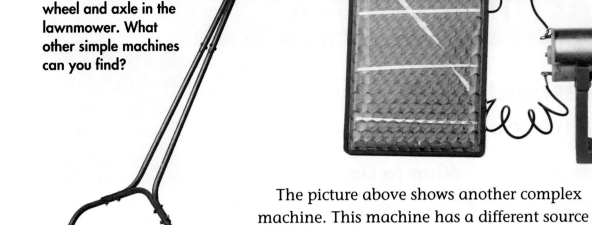

You can easily see one wheel and axle in the lawnmower. What other simple machines can you find?

The picture above shows another complex machine. This machine has a different source of power than the can opener. Instead of your muscle power, this machine uses solar energy, or energy from sunlight. The box on the left is filled with solar cells. They change the energy of the Sun's rays into electricity that the machine can use.

Now look carefully at the other parts of the machine. You will see some simple machines.

There is more than one wheel and axle. Can you find them? You will also see some gears. Can you tell how two gears are changing the direction of motion?

The machine is lifting a load. Does the lifting part remind you of a simple machine? What is it?

This machine has wheels and axles and a pulley. It may have some other simple machines that you aren't able to see.

Do you see more than one wheel and axle in the eggbeater? What other simple machines do you see?

✓ **Lesson Checkpoint**

1. Name three kinds of work that a screw can do. Give an example of each.
2. What is a complex machine?
3. ⊙ **Summarize** what you know about a can opener.

Investigate What tasks can a machine do?

Materials

safety goggles

common objects

What to Do

1 Plan a device to do a task. Your device could make a toy car move, push a marble, make noise, or lift something. Or make a device to do something else.

What materials and tools did you use?

2 Think about how your task could be done. Design and build a device made of 2 or more simple machines to do your task. Describe your device. **Predict** whether your device will do its task.

3 Test your prediction. **Investigate** how well your device does the task. Investigate what might have caused problems.

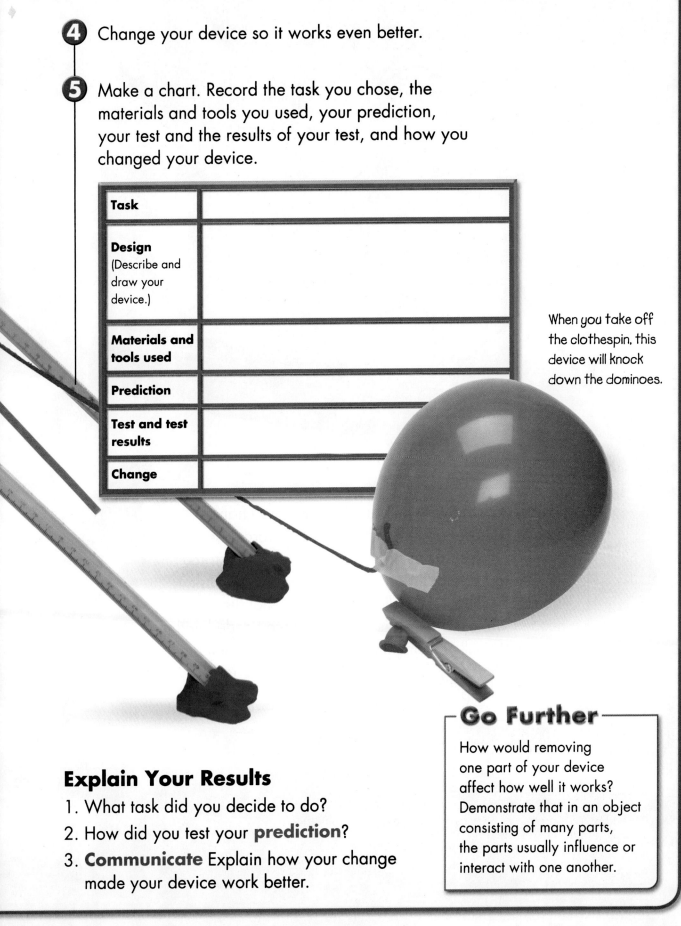

4 Change your device so it works even better.

5 Make a chart. Record the task you chose, the materials and tools you used, your prediction, your test and the results of your test, and how you changed your device.

Task	
Design (Describe and draw your device.)	
Materials and tools used	
Prediction	
Test and test results	
Change	

When you take off the clothespin, this device will knock down the dominoes.

Explain Your Results

1. What task did you decide to do?
2. How did you test your **prediction**?
3. **Communicate** Explain how your change made your device work better.

Go Further

How would removing one part of your device affect how well it works? Demonstrate that in an object consisting of many parts, the parts usually influence or interact with one another.

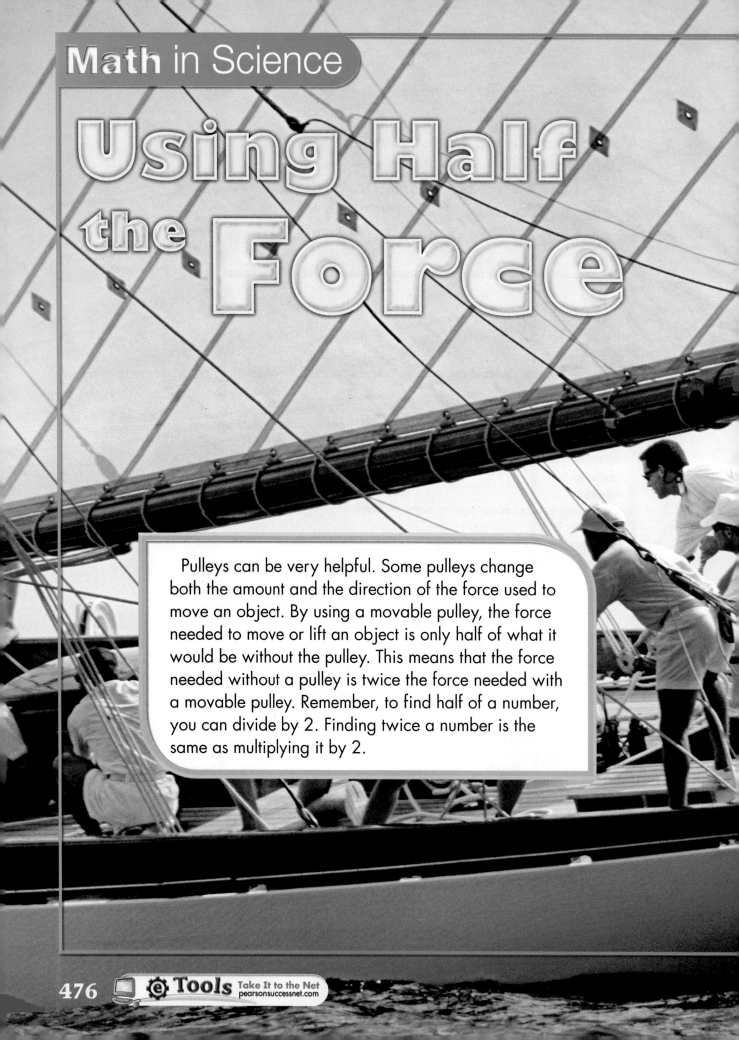

Using Half the Force

Pulleys can be very helpful. Some pulleys change both the amount and the direction of the force used to move an object. By using a movable pulley, the force needed to move or lift an object is only half of what it would be without the pulley. This means that the force needed without a pulley is twice the force needed with a movable pulley. Remember, to find half of a number, you can divide by 2. Finding twice a number is the same as multiplying it by 2.

e Tools Take It to the Net
pearsonsuccessnet.com

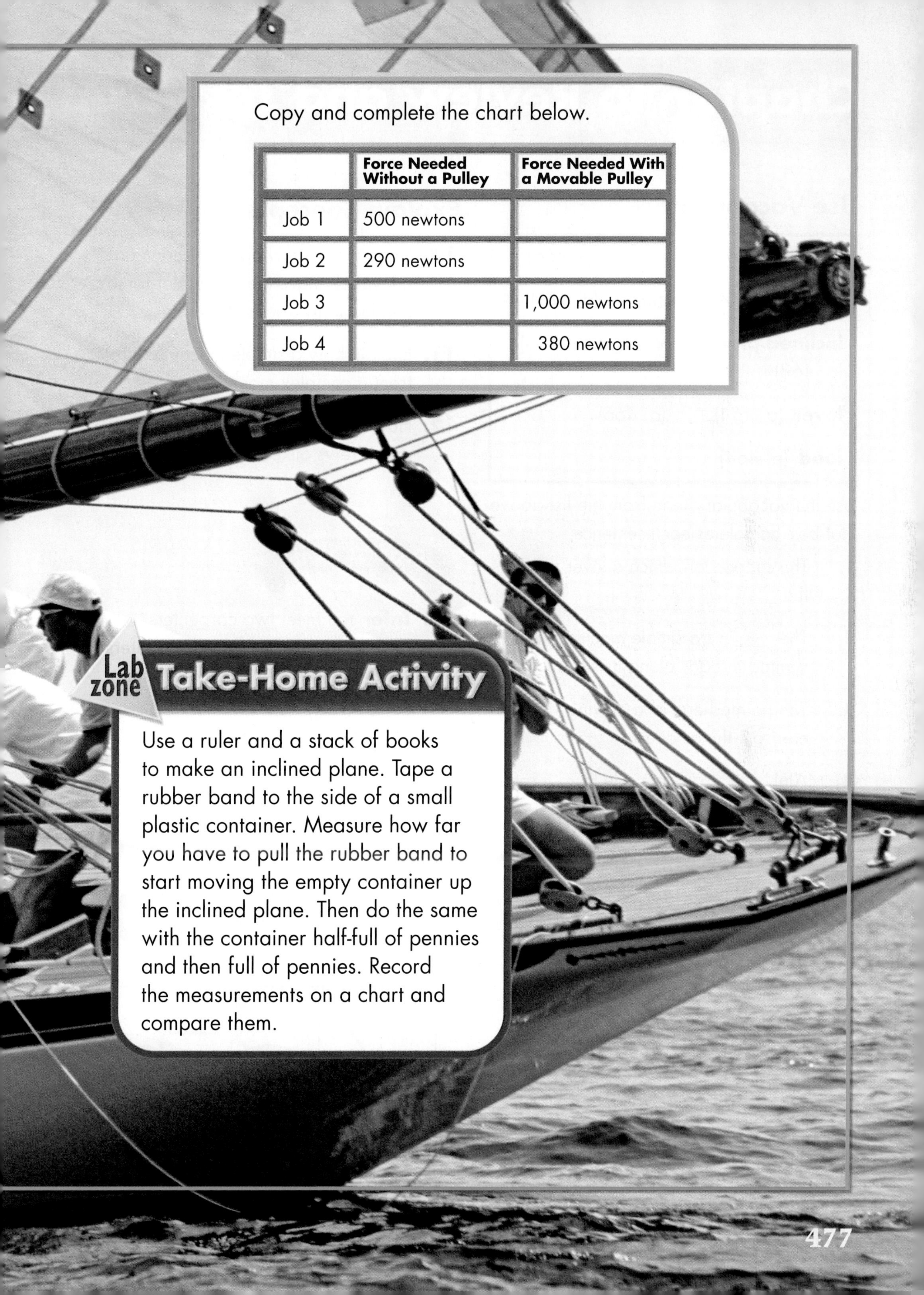

Copy and complete the chart below.

	Force Needed Without a Pulley	Force Needed With a Movable Pulley
Job 1	500 newtons	
Job 2	290 newtons	
Job 3		1,000 newtons
Job 4		380 newtons

Lab zone Take-Home Activity

Use a ruler and a stack of books to make an inclined plane. Tape a rubber band to the side of a small plastic container. Measure how far you have to pull the rubber band to start moving the empty container up the inclined plane. Then do the same with the container half-full of pennies and then full of pennies. Record the measurements on a chart and compare them.

Chapter 16 Review and Test Prep

Use Vocabulary

effort (p. 464)	**pulley** (p. 466)
fulcrum (p. 464)	**screw** (p. 471)
inclined plane (p. 468)	**wedge** (p. 470)
	wheel and axle (p. 466)
lever (p. 464)	
load (p. 464)	

Use the vocabulary term from the list above that best completes each sentence.

1. The support on which a lever rests is the _____.

2. The _____ is a simple machine with slanted threads along its sides.

3. The pointed end of a moving _____ can split things apart.

4. A(n) _____ can be made from a rope and wheel or a chain and wheel.

5. The _____ is a push or squeeze that makes a lever move.

6. A windup key on a toy is an example of a _____.

7. A wheelchair ramp is a type of _____.

8. A baseball bat is a kind of _____.

9. In a simple machine, a weight to be lifted or moved is the _____.

Explain Concepts

10. Explain how moving the fulcrum on a lever changes the amount of force needed to move an object.

11. Explain how a simple machine differs from a complex machine.

12. How are inclined planes, wedges, and screws alike?

Process Skills

13. **Infer** You meet two carpenters. One uses nails, but the other prefers screws. Write one possible reason for each carpenter's choice.

14. **Classify** each picture as a simple machine or a complex machine.

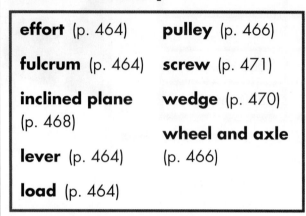

# Summarize

15. Make a graphic organizer like the one shown below. Write three details about levers. Use them to summarize what you know about levers.

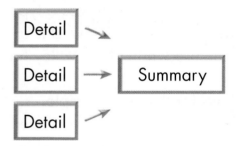

# Test Prep

Choose the letter that best completes the statement or answers the question.

16. In science, *work* means
  Ⓐ using force to move or change something.
  Ⓑ how far something moves.
  Ⓒ doing a job.
  Ⓓ how hard you push on something.

17. Which object is NOT a lever?
  Ⓕ a pair of scissors
  Ⓖ a nutcracker
  Ⓗ a gear
  Ⓘ a crowbar

18. A gently sloping driveway on a hill is
  Ⓐ a wedge.
  Ⓑ a pulley.
  Ⓒ a lever.
  Ⓓ an inclined plane.

19. Explain why the answer you chose for Question 16 is the best. For each of the answers you did not choose, give a reason why it is not the best choice.

20. **Writing in Science** **Expository**
Suppose someone you know has never seen a pair of scissors. You want to explain how to use the scissors and what is happening when they cut. Using what you know about simple machines, write a paragraph that tells this person how scissors work.

Archimedes

Archimedes was perhaps the greatest scientist of the ancient world. He was born about 287 B.C. in Syracuse, a Greek colony in Sicily. Archimedes and King Hielo II of Syracuse were friends. They may have been related. Archimedes probably studied in Alexandria, Egypt. Historians think that while he lived in Egypt, he invented a device that could raise water from the Nile River to irrigate nearby farmland. The device, which was a type of auger, became known as Archimedes' Screw. It is a simple machine that has been used in the Nile Valley for thousands of years.

Archimedes discovered laws for the use of simple machines such as levers and screws. He also developed many complex machines. Some were weapons used in battle. Others were devices that could move heavy loads. One device was a system of pulleys that could raise and move a whole ship—even a ship with passengers on it! In explaining how the lever can be used, he is said to have told King Hielo, "Give me a place to stand on, and I will move the entire Earth."

Lab zone Take-Home Activity

Make a list of objects in your home that have pulleys, wheels, screws, levers, wedges, or inclined planes.

Unit C Test Talk

Use Information from Text and Graphics

Sometimes information that you need is given in a graphic organizer, a table, a graph, or some other display. Once you understand exactly what the display shows, you can decide how to use it. Then, by adding new facts to the facts you already know, you can answer the questions.

In a graph or a table, look for a pattern to see how the data compare. A pattern can also help you estimate the answer. If the data are in a table or chart, changing the order of the items may make the new information easier to use.

Read the passage. Then use the data in the table to answer the questions.

One substance may sink under or float on top of another substance. To decide what happens, compare the density of the two substances. Density is mass divided by volume. The substance with the greater density sinks under the other substance.

Substance	Density at 20°C
Corn oil	0.93
Corn syrup	1.38
Gold	19.32
Honey	1.4
Lead	11.35
Mayonnaise	0.91
Milk	1.03
Piece of apple	0.6
Salt	2.16
Water	1.00

Use What You Know

Suppose a sample of each substance were put into the same container. Use the information in the table to answer the questions about what would happen.

1. Which would float at the top?
   - Ⓐ corn oil
   - Ⓑ mayonnaise
   - Ⓒ piece of apple
   - Ⓓ water

2. Which is the best explanation why the two substances might be hard to tell apart in the container?
   - Ⓕ Corn syrup and corn oil are both made from corn.
   - Ⓖ Gold and a piece of apple are both solids.
   - Ⓗ Honey and corn oil are both golden colored.
   - Ⓘ Milk and water have about the same density.

3. How would you arrange the items to make the information easier to use?
   - Ⓐ Keep the items in alphabetical order.
   - Ⓑ List all of the liquids first.
   - Ⓒ List all of the solids first.
   - Ⓓ List items in order of their densities.

4. Suppose you make a bar graph from the data. Which substances would have bars that were almost the same length?
   - Ⓕ corn oil and mayonnaise
   - Ⓖ gold and lead
   - Ⓗ milk and honey
   - Ⓘ piece of apple and salt

481

Unit C Wrap-Up

Chapter 11

How can matter be compared, measured, and combined?

- We use tools to measure the mass and volume of matter.
- Observations and measurements help us compare matter.
- Physical and chemical changes can happen when matter is combined.

Chapter 12

How does heat energy move from one object to another?

- Heat energy can move from one object to another by conduction.
- Heat moves through liquids and gases in a pattern called convection.
- Energy from the Sun comes to Earth by radiation.

Chapter 13

What are some ways that energy can be changed from one type to another?

- Electric charges can move through wire as electric current. Current moving through a light bulb produces light and heat.
- Electric current produces magnetic fields.

Chapter 14

How do sound and light travel?

- Sound travels in waves through solids, liquids, and gases.
- Light travels as electromagnetic waves.

Chapter 15

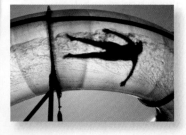

What causes motion and how does it affect us?

- Forces start objects moving, speed them up, slow them down, stop them, or change their direction.
- Changes in motion require force.

Chapter 16

How do simple machines make work easier?
- Simple machines change the direction in which a force is applied.
- Simple machines can also change the amount of force you need to apply.

Performance Assessment

Height and Potential Energy

Find out if the height of an object affects its potential energy. Use modeling clay to make three balls of the same size. Place a ball in a plastic bag and put it on the floor. Hold a thick book flat above the ball. Release the book so that it lands on the clay. Remove the flattened ball from the bag and trace its outline on a sheet of paper. Repeat the procedure using the other balls of clay. Drop the book from different heights. Record your procedures and your observations. Based on your observations, draw a conclusion about height and potential energy.

Read More About Physical Science

Look for books like these in the library.

A force is needed to move the snow.

Experiment How is motion affected by mass?

A force can cause an object to move. In this **experiment** you will find out how the mass of an object affects the distance the object will move.

Materials

$\frac{1}{2}$ of a cup and marble

2 metric rulers

2 books

4 pennies and tape

balance and gram cubes

calculator or computer (optional)

Process Skills

You **experiment** when you carry out a fair test of your **hypothesis**.

Ask a question.

How does the mass of a cup affect the distance a rolling marble will move the cup?

State a hypothesis.

If the mass of a cup is increased, then will the distance the cup is moved by a rolling marble increase, decrease, or remain the same? Write your **hypothesis**.

Identify and control variables.

You will increase the mass of the cup by taping pennies to the cup. You will **measure** the distance the cup moves. Everything else must remain the same.

Test your hypothesis.

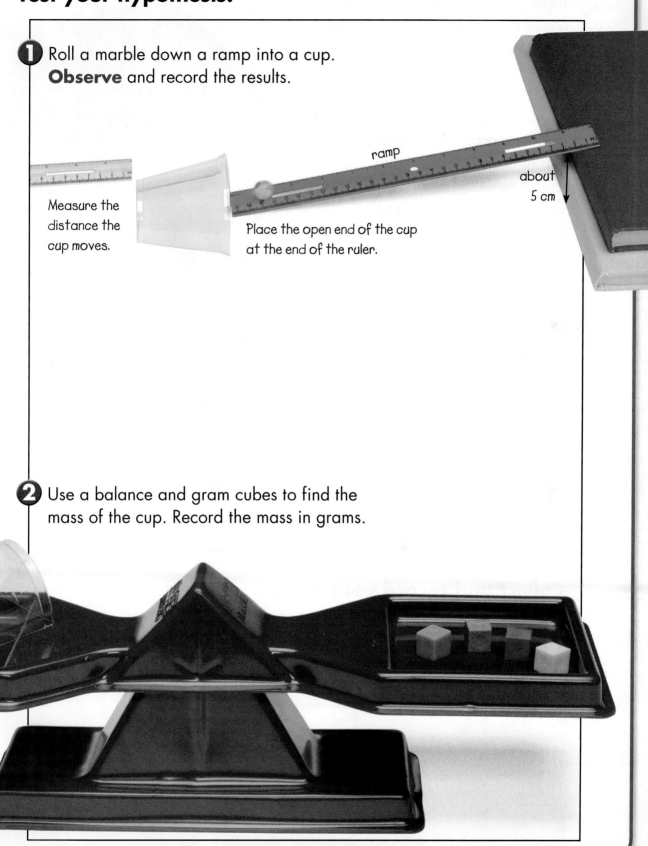

1 Roll a marble down a ramp into a cup.
Observe and record the results.

ramp

about
5 cm

Measure the
distance the
cup moves.

Place the open end of the cup
at the end of the ruler.

2 Use a balance and gram cubes to find the
mass of the cup. Record the mass in grams.

485

3 Tape a penny on top of the cup. Move the cup back to the end of the ramp.

4 Roll the marble down the ramp into the cup. Record the results. Then find the mass of the cup with the penny taped on it. Record the mass.

5 Repeat using 2, 3, and 4 pennies.

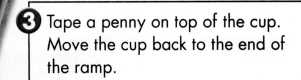

penny taped on cup

Collect and record your data.

Number of Pennies	Distance Cup Moved (cm)	Mass of Cup with Pennies (g)
0		
1		
2		
3		
4		

Make a table to record your data.

More Lab zone Activities Take It to the Net pearsonsuccessnet.com

Explain your data.

Use your data to make a line graph. Look at your graph closely. Describe how the distance the cup moved was affected by the mass of the cup with pennies.

Your teacher may wish you to use a computer (with the right software) or a graphing calculator to help collect, organize, analyze, and present your data. These tools can help you make tables, charts, and graphs.

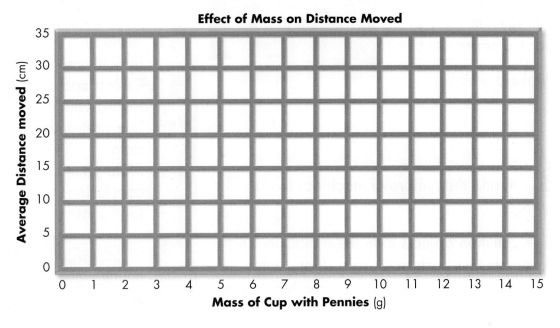

Effect of Mass on Distance Moved

Average Distance moved (cm)

Mass of Cup with Pennies (g)

You may wish to use graph paper.

Based on the data and the pattern shown by your line graph, predict the distance the cup would move with 5 pennies.

State your conclusion.

Explain how mass affects the distance that the cup moves. Compare your hypothesis with your results. **Communicate** your conclusion.

Go Further

How would changing the height of the ramp affect how the cup moves? Design and carry out a plan to investigate this or other questions you may have. Make sure to write a procedure others can understand and use to repeat your experiment.

A Pinhole Camera

A camera uses light to form images on photographic paper.

Idea: Make a pinhole camera.

Build a Better Door Opener

People invent and then improve machines to do different jobs.

Idea: Use common objects to make a machine that will do a simple task such as close a door, water plants, crack an egg, or open a window. Name the machine and design a box or container to package it. Make a diagram with labels to show all the simple machines included in the new machine.

Battery Power

Like other power sources, batteries have different life spans.

Idea: Use several different brands of batteries. You will need a flashlight for each brand. Make sure that the flashlights all have the same type of bulb and use the same number of batteries. Turn on all of the flashlights, and time how long each battery brand keeps the flashlight lit.

Using Scientific Methods

1. Ask a question.
2. State a hypothesis.
3. Identify and control variables.
4. Test your hypothesis.
5. Collect and record your data.
6. Interpret your data.
7. State your conclusion.
8. Go further.

Metric and Customary Measurement

The metric system is the measurement system most commonly used in science. Metric units are sometimes called SI units. SI stands for International System. It is called that because these units are used around the world.

These prefixes are used in the metric system:

kilo- means *thousand*
1 kilometer equals 1,000 meters

milli- means *one thousandth*
1,000 millimeters equals 1 meter or 1 millimeter = 0.001 meter

centi- means *one hundredth*
100 centimeters equals 1 meter or 1 centimeter = 0.01 meter

Length and Distance

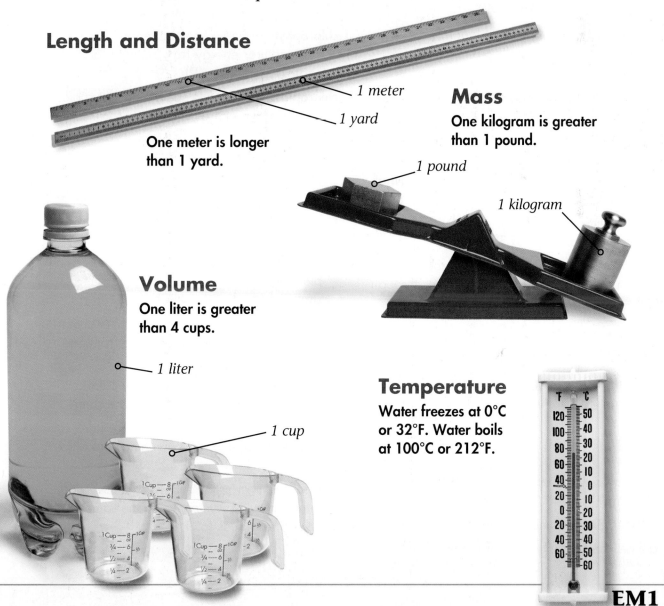

1 meter

1 yard

One meter is longer than 1 yard.

Mass

One kilogram is greater than 1 pound.

1 pound

1 kilogram

Volume

One liter is greater than 4 cups.

1 liter

1 cup

Temperature

Water freezes at 0°C or 32°F. Water boils at 100°C or 212°F.

Glossary

The glossary uses letters and signs to show how words are pronounced. The mark ′ is placed after a syllable with a primary or heavy accent. The mark ′ is placed after a syllable with a secondary or lighter acdcent.

To hear these words pronounced, listen to the AudioText CD.

absorption (ab sôrp′shən) the taking in of light energy by an object (p. 420)

adaptation (ad′ap tā′shən) trait that helps a living thing survive in its environment (p. 26)

anemometer (an′ə mom′ə tər) a tool that measures wind speed (p. 195)

astronomy (ə stron′ə mē) the study of planets, stars, and other objects in space (p. 519)

atmosphere (at′mə sfir) the blanket of gases that surrounds Earth (p. 188)

atom (at′əm) one of the tiny particles that make up all of matter (p. 375)

axis (ak′sis) an imaginary line that goes through an object; Earth's axis goes through the North and South Poles (p. 496)

barometer (bə rom′ə tər) a tool that measures air pressure (p. 194)

carnivores (kär′nə vôrz) consumers that eat only animals (p. 84)

cause (kȯz) why something happens (p. 109)

cell (sel) the building block of life (p. 7)

change of state (chānj ov stāt) physical change in matter caused by a different arrangement or movement of particles (p. 320)

chemical change (kem′ə kəl chānj) a change that results in a new substance (p. 336)

chlorophyll (klôr′ə fil) green material in plants that captures energy from sunlight for photosynthesis (p. 49)

chloroplast (klôr′ə plast) a special part of a plant that traps the energy in sunlight for making food (p. 8)

classifying (klas′ə fī ing) arranging or sorting objects, events, or living things according to their properties (p. 34)

collecting data (kə lekt′ing dā′tə) gathering observations and measurements (p. 108)

communicating (kə myü′nə kāt ing) using words, pictures, charts, graphs, and diagrams to share information (p. 180)

communication (kə myü′nə kā′shən) the process of sending any type of message from one place to another (p. 556)

community (kə myü′nə tē) different populations that interact with each other in the same area (p. 82)

compare (kəm pâr′) to say how things are alike (p. 5)

competition (kom′pə tish′ən) two or more living things in an ecosystem using the same limited resources (p. 114)

compression (kəm presh′ən) the pushing together of a mass so that it occupies less space (p. 408)

conclusion (kən klü′zhən) a decision reached after thinking about facts and details (p. 45)

condensation (kon′den sā′shən) the process of water vapor, a gas, changing to a liquid (p. 187)

conduction (kən duk′shən) the transfer or passing of energy (p. 354)

conductor (kən duk′tər) a material that allows thermal energy or electricity to pass through it (p. 354)

conservation (kon′sər vā′shən) using only what you need as efficiently as possible (p. 296)

constellation (kon′stə lā′shən) any one of 88 areas in the sky that are used to identify and name the stars (p. 504)

consumer (kən sü′mər) living things that eat other organisms (p. 84)

contrast (kən trast′) to say how things are different (p. 5)

convection current (kən vek′shən kėr′ənt) the pattern in which thermal energy flows; formed when heated liquid or gas expands and is less dense than a cooler liquid or gas around it (p. 356)

crater (krā′tər) a large hole shaped like a bowl in the surface of Earth, another planet, a moon, or other object in space (p. 270)

cytoplasm (sī′tə plaz′əm) a gel-like liquid inside the cell membrane that contains the things that the cell needs (p. 8)

decomposers (dē′kəm pō′zərz) organisms that live and grow by breaking down the waste and remains of dead plants and animals to obtain nutrients (p. 87)

density (den′sə tē) the property of matter that compares the mass of an object to its volume (p. 326)

deposition (dep′ə zish′ən) the laying down of rock, soil, organic matter, or other material on the surface of Earth (p. 267)

details (di tālz′) individual pieces of information that support a main idea (p. 213)

dormant (dôr′mənt) in a state of rest (p. 62)

dwarf planet (dwôrf plan′it) small, ball-shaped object that revolves around the Sun (p. 536)

earthquake (ėrth′kwāk′) a shaking of Earth's crust or lithosphere caused by sudden, shifting movements in the crust (p. 272)

eclipse (i klips′) a temporary situation in which an object in space casts its shadow on another object (p. 502)

ecosystem (ē′kō sis′təm) all the living and nonliving things in an environment and the many ways they interact (p. 79)

effect (ə feckt′) what happens as a result of a cause (p. 109)

effort (ef′ərt) the force used on a simple machine (p. 464)

electric current (i lek′trik kėr′ənt) the flow of an electric charge through a material (p. 378)

electromagnet (i lek′trō mag′nit) a coil of wire that causes a magnetic field when current moves through the wire (p. 387)

element (el′ə mənt) matter that has only one kind of atom (p. 337)

ellipse (i lips′) an oval-shaped curve that is like a circle stretched out in opposite directions (p. 498)

endangered (en dān′jərd) a species whose population has been reduced to such small numbers that it is in danger of becoming extinct (p. 120)

energy (en′ər jē) the ability to do work or to cause a change (p. 84)

energy transfer (en′ər jē tran′sfėr′) the flow of energy in a food chain from the producer to prey to predator (p. 86)

environment (en vī′rən mənt) everything that surrounds a living thing (p. 118)

epicenter (ep′ə sen′tər) the point on Earth's surface directly above the focus of an earthquake (p. 272)

equator (i kwā′tər) the imaginary line that separates the northern and southern halves of Earth (p. 499)

erosion (i rō′zhən) the moving of pieces of soil or rock by mechanisms including gravity, wind, water, ice, or plants or animals (p. 266)

estimating and measuring (es′tə māt ing and mezh′ər ing) telling how large you think an object is and then finding out its exact size (p. 308)

evaporation (i vap′ə rā′shən) the change from liquid water to water vapor (p. 186)

experiment (ek sper′ə mənt) to formulate and test a hypothesis using a scientific method (p. 172)

explore (ek splôr′) to study a scientific idea in a hands-on manner (p. 4)

extinct (ek stingkt′) no longer living, as an entire species, or no longer active, as a volcano (p. 120)

fault (fôlt) a break or crack in Earth where the rocks on one side have moved relative to the rocks on the other side (p. 272)

fertilization (fèr′tl ə zā′shən) the process by which an egg cell and a sperm cell combine (p. 56)

food chain (füd chān) the process by which energy moves from one type of living thing to another (p. 86)

food web (füd web) a system of overlapping food chains in which the flow of energy branches out in many directions (p. 88)

force (fôrs) any push or pull (p. 442)

forming questions and hypotheses (fôrm′ing kwes′chənz and hī poth′ə səz′) thinking of how you can solve a problem or answer a question (p. 484)

fossil (fos′əl) remains or mark of a living thing from long ago (p. 244)

fossil fuels (fos′əl fyü′əlz) fuels including coal, petroleum, and natural gas that are made from fossils, or the remains of living things that died millions of years ago (p. 294)

frame of reference (frām uv ref′ər əns) objects that don't seem to move define your frame of reference (p. 440)

frequency (frē′kwən sē) the number of times a wave makes a complete cycle in a second (p. 409)

friction (frik′shən) force that acts when two surfaces rub together (p. 445)

front (frunt) the boundary across which two different air masses touch another (p. 191)

fulcrum (ful′krəm) the support on which a lever plus its load rests (p. 464)

galaxy (gal′ək sē) system of millions to trillions of stars held together by the force of gravity (p. 519)

gas (gas) one of the states of matter which takes the shape of its container and expands to whatever space is available (p. 321)

genus (jē′nəs) a grouping that contains similar, closely related animals (p. 12)

gravity (grav′ə tē) a force of attraction between two or more objects over a distance. The more mass an object has, the stronger the gravitational force. (p. 521)

habitat (hab′ə tat) area or place where an organism lives in an ecosystem (p. 82)

hazardous waste (haz′ər dəs wāst) substances that are very harmful to humans and other organisms (p. 126)

heat (hēt) the transfer of thermal energy between matter with different temperatures (p. 354)

herbivores (ėr′bə vôrz) consumers that get energy by eating only plants (p. 84)

host (hōst) an organism that is harmed by a parasite (p. 117)

humidity (hyü mid′ə tē) the amount of water vapor in the air (p. 190)

humus (hyü′məs) a dark brown part of soil that is made up of decomposed plants and animals (p. 289)

hurricane (hėr′ə kān) a dangerous storm made up of swirling bands of thunderstorms with wind speeds of at least 119 km per hour (p. 215)

identifying and controlling variables (ī den′tə fī ing and kən trōl′ing vâr′ē ə bəlz) changing one thing, but keep all the other factors the same (p. 172)

igneous rock (ig′nē əs rok′) rock that forms from molten (melted) rock (p. 246)

immune system (i myün′ sis′təm) the organs in your body that defend against disease (p. 161)

inclined plane (in klīnd′ plān) a simple machine like a ramp (p. 12)

infectious disease (in fek′shəs də zēz′) a disease that can pass from one organism to another (p. 158)

inferring (in fėr′ing) drawing a conclusion or making a reasonable guess based on what you have learned or what you know (p. 66)

insulator (in′sə lā′tər) a material or substance that limits the amount of heat that passes through it (p. 355)

interpreting data (in tėr′prit ing dā′tə) using the information you have collected to solve problems or answer questions (p. 200)

invertebrates (in vėr′tə brits) animals without backbones (p. 22)

investigate (in ves′tə gāt) to solve a problem or answer a question by following an existing procedure or an original one (p. 96)

investigating and experimenting (in ves′tə gāt ing and ek sper′ə ment ing) planning and doing an investigation to test a hypothesis or solve a problem (p. 484)

involuntary muscles (in vol′ən ter′ē mus′əlz) muscles that you cannot control (p. 146)

kinetic energy (kin net′ik en′ər jē) energy of motion (p. 448)

landform (land′fôrm′) a natural feature on Earth's surface; landforms include mountains, hills, valleys, plains, plateaus, and coastal features (p. 263)

landslide (land′slīd) a rapid downhill movement of large amounts of rock and soil (p. 268)

lever (lev′ər) a simple machine made of a bar resting on a fulcrum (p. 464)

life cycle (līf sī′kəl) the various stages through which an organism passes from birth as it grows, matures, and dies (p. 20)

light (līt) a form of energy that travels in waves and can affect properties of matter (p. 418)

liquid (lik′wid) one of the states of matter which does not have a definite shape but takes up a definite amount of space (p. 321)

load (lōd) the weight that is to be lifted or moved (p. 464)

lunar eclipse (lü′nər i klips′) the passage of the Moon through Earth's shadow (p. 502)

luster (lus′tər) the way a mineral's surface reflects light (p. 240)

magnetic field (mag net′ik fēld) the invisible force that loops between the poles of a magnet due to the arrangement of charges. The force is strongest at the poles, or ends, and gets weaker as distance from the magnet increases. (p. 382)

magnetism (mag′nə tiz′əm) the property of attraction of an object that has a magnetic field. It can attract other objects made of certain metals. (p. 382)

main ideas (mān i dē′əz) the most important information in a reading passage (p. 213)

making and using models (māk′ing and yüz′ing mod′lz) making a model from materials or making a sketch or a diagram (p. 162)

making operational definitions (māk′ing op′ər ā′shə nəl def′ə nish′ənz) defining or describing an object or event based on your own experience with it (p. 394)

mass (mas) amount of matter in an object (p. 322)

matter (mat′ər) anything that takes up space and has mass (p. 320)

metamorphic rock (met′ə môr′fik rok′) rock that has changed as a result of heating and pressure (p. 248)

meteorologist (mē′tē ə rol′ə jist) a scientist who studies and measures weather conditions (p. 194)

mineral (min′ər əl) natural, nonliving solid crystal that makes up rocks (p. 239)

mixture (miks′chər) a combination of two or more substances that keep their individual properties (p. 328)

moon (mün) a satellite of a planet (p. 524)

Moon phase (mün fāz) the different shapes of the Moon between the time a full Moon is visible and the time when no part of the Moon is visible (p. 501)

neuron (nür′ron) basic working unit of the nervous system; the nerve cell (p. 154)

niche (nich) the specific role an organism has in its habitat (p. 82)

nonrenewable resources (non′ri nü′ə bəl rē′sôrs əz) resource supplies that exist in limited amounts or are used much faster than they can be replaced in nature (p. 294)

nucleus (nü′klē əs) the control center of a cell (p. 8)

observing (əb zėrv′ing) using your senses to find out about objects, events, or living things (p. 4)

omnivores (om′nə vôrz′) consumers that eat both plants and animals (p. 84)

opaque (ō pāk′) describes materials that do not let any light pass through them (p. 421)

optical fibers (op′tə kəl fi′bərz) very thin tubes that allow light to pass through them; often used by doctors in medical procedures (p. 554)

orbit (ôr′bit) the path followed by one object as it revolves around another object, such as Earth's orbit around the Sun (p. 498)

ore (ôr) a mineral-rich rock deposit that can be removed from Earth's crust and used to make products (p. 294)

organ (ôr′gən) a group of tissues working together to carry out body processes (p. 143)

organism (ôr′gə niz′əm) the highest level of cell organization (p. 8)

ovary (ō′vər ē) the thick bottom part of the pistil where the egg cells are stored (p. 56)

parallel circuits (par′ə lel sėr′kits) two or more paths in which an electric charge can flow (p. 381)

parasite (par′ə sīt) an organism that lives on or in another organism, helping itself but hurting the other organism (p. 117)

pathogens (path′ə jənz) organisms that cause disease (p. 158)

petroleum (pə trō′lē əm) a crude oil that is found in rocks; a nonrenewable energy source (p. 294)

photosynthesis (fō′tō sin′thə sis) the process in which plants make their own food (p. 48)

physical change (fiz′ə kəl chānj) a change in the size, shape, or state of matter (p. 332)

pistil (pis′tl) a female structure in plants that produces egg cells (p. 55)

pitch (pich) a measure of whether a sound seems high or low, determined by the sound's frequency (p. 412)

planet (plan′it) a very large, ball-shaped object that moves around a star, such as the Sun (p. 520)

pollution (pə lü′shən) waste from products made or used by people (p. 124)

population (pop′yə lā′shən) all the members of one species that live within an area of an ecosystem (p. 82)

potential energy (pə ten′shəl en′ər jē) the amount of energy available to do work because of the way a system is arranged (p. 448)

precipitation (pri sip′ə tā′shən) any form of water falling from the air to Earth's surface (p. 187)

predator (pred′ə tər) a consumer that hunts other animals for food (p. 28)

predict (pri dikt′) make a statement about what might happen next (p. 517)

predicting (pri dikt′ing) telling what you think will happen (p. 66)

prey (prā) any animal hunted by others for food (p. 86)

producer (prə dü′sər) living thing that makes its own food (p. 84)

protist (prō′tist) one-cell organism with a nucleus and other cell parts (p. 11)

pulley (pùl′ē) a simple machine made of a wheel with a rope around it (p. 467)

radiation (rā′dē ā′shən) the transmission of energy as light (p. 358)

recycling (rē sī′kling) saving, collecting, or using materials again instead of turning them into waste (p. 297)

reflection (ri flek′shən) the bouncing back of a wave off an object or surface (p. 420)

refraction (ri frak′shən) bending of a wave caused by the change of speed that occurs when the wave passes from one medium into another (p. 422)

relative motion (rel′ə tiv mō′shən) change in position of one object compared to the position of some fixed object (p. 439)

renewable resource (ri nü′ə bəl ri sôrs′) resource that is endless, such as sunlight, or that is naturally replaced in a fairly short time, such as trees (p. 287)

resistance (ri zis′təns) a quality of an object which means that electric current cannot flow easily through it (p. 379)

resource (rē′sôrs) an important material that living things need (p. 287)

revolution (rev′ə lü′shən) the repeated motion of one object around another, much more massive object; for instance, the motion of Earth around the Sun (p. 498)

rotation (rō tā′shən) the spinning of a planet, moon, or star around its axis (p. 496)

satellite (sat′l it) something that orbits a planet (p. 524)

scientific method (sī′ən tif′ik meth′əd) organized steps in solving problems (p. xxvi)

screw (skrü) a simple machine made of a stick with ridges wrapped around it (p. 471)

sediment (sed′ə mənt) any earth material that has been moved from one place to another and laid down on the surface of Earth. It includes material moved by gravity, wind, water, ice, or animals and plants. (p. 242)

sedimentary rock (sed′ə men′tər ē rok′) rock that forms when sediments are cemented together and harden (p. 242)

sepal (sē′pəl) one of several leaf-like parts that cover and protect the flower bud (p. 55)

sequence (sē′kwəns) the order in which things happen (p. 77)

series circuit (sir′ēz sėr′kit) a simple circular path in which an electric current flows only one way through each part of that circuit (p. 380)

solar cells (sō′lər selz) electric cells that convert the Sun's energy into electricity (p. 293)

solar eclipse (sō′lər i klips′) the passage of the Moon between the Sun and Earth; the Moon casts its shadow on Earth (p. 503)

solar energy (sō′lər en′ər jē) the energy transformed from sunlight (p. 287)

solar system (sō′lər sis′təm) a system of planets and other objects that move around the Sun (p. 520)

solid (sol′id) matter that has a definite shape and usually takes up a definite amount of space (p. 321)

solubility (sol′yə bil′ə tē) ability of one substance to dissolve in another (p. 331)

solute (sol′yüt) the substance that is dissolved in a solution (p. 330)

solution (sə lü′shən) a combination of two or more substances where one is dissolved by the other (p. 330)

solvent (sol′vənt) the substance that dissolves another substance in a solution (p. 330)

space probe (spās prōb) a vehicle that carries cameras and other tools for studying distant objects in space (p. 522)

species (spē′shēz) a group of similar organisms that can mate and produce offspring that can reproduce (p. 12)

speed (spēd) the rate at which an object's position changes (p. 440)

stamen (stā′mən) male structure in plants that makes pollen (p. 55)

star (stär) a giant ball of hot, glowing gases (p. 495)

static electricity (stat′ik i lek′tris′ə tē) the imbalance of positive or negative charges between objects (p. 375)

storm surge (stôrm sėrj) water pushed ahead onto shore by the winds outside the eye wall of a hurricane (p. 219)

succession (sək sesh′ən) gradual change from one community of organisms to another (p. 118)

summarize (sum′ə riz′) give only the main points (p. 337)

summary (sum′ə rē) a short retelling of something read (p. 237)

Sun (sun) the star that is the central and largest body in the our solar system (p. 521)

system (sis′təm) a set of parts that interact with one another (p. 79)

technology (tek nol′ə jē) the knowledge, processes, and products that we use to solve problems and make our lives easier (p. 551)

telecommunications (tel′ə kə myü′nə kā′shənz) communications sent by telephone, television, satellite, and radio (p. 557)

thermal energy (thėr′məl en′ər jē) total energy of motion of particles in a system (p. 351)

tissue (tish′ü) a group of one type of cell (p. 8)

tornado (tôr nā′dō) a rapidly spinning column of air that comes down out of a cloud and touches the ground (p. 222)

translucent (tranz lü′snt) describes materials that let some light rays pass through but scatter some of the other rays (p. 421)

transparent (tran spâr′ənt) describes materials that let nearly all the light rays that hit them pass through (p. 421)

tropical depression (trop′ə kəl di presh′ən) a low pressure air mass that forms over warm water and has swirling winds can be as strong as 61 km per hour (p. 216)

tropical storm (trop′ə kəl stôrm) a low pressure air mass that forms over warm water and has swirling winds that are more than 61 kph but less than 119 kph (p. 216)

universe (yü′nə vėrs′) all of the objects that exist in space (p. 519)

vaccine (vak sēn′) an injection of dead or weakened pathogens that causes you to be immune to a disease (p. 161)

vehicle (vē′ə kəl) something that carries people and objects from one place to another such as automobiles, trucks, trains, ships, airplanes, and rockets (p. 558)

velocity (və los′ə tē) the speed and the direction an object is moving (p. 441)

vertebrates (vėr′tə brits) animals with backbones (p. 18)

volcano (vol kā′nō) a cone-shaped landform that sometimes releases hot rocks, gases, and ashes (p. 270)

volume (vol′yəm) amount of space matter takes up (p. 324)

voluntary muscles (vol′ən ter′ē mus′əlz) muscles that you can control (p. 146)

vortex (vôr′teks) a spinning, funnel-shaped area in a fluid (p. 223)

water cycle (wȯ′tər sī′kəl) the movement of water from Earth's surface into the air and back again; includes evaporation, condensation and precipitation (p. 186)

wavelength (wāv′lengkth) distance between one point on a wave to the next similar point on a wave (p. 409)

weathering (weᴛʜ′ər ing) a gradual wearing away or changing of rock and soil caused by water, ice, temperature changes, wind, chemicals, or living things (p. 264)

wedge (wej) a simple machine that is made of two inclined planes put together and that can be driven into another material (p. 470)

wheel and axle (wēl and ak′səl) a simple machine made of a wheel and a rod joined to the center of the wheel (p. 466)

wind vane (wind vān) a tool that shows the direction from which the wind is blowing (p. 195)

work (wėrk) using force in order to move an object a certain distance (p. 448)

Index

This index lists the pages on which topics appear in this book. Page numbers after a *p* refer to a photograph or drawing. Page numbers after a *c* refer to a chart, graph, or diagram.

549, 553, 559, 565

Predict, 517, 527, 537, 543

Sequence, *77, 87, 95, 101, 437, 439, 443, 455*

Summarize, 237, 239, 241, 243, 245, 255, 461, 467, 473, 479

Tarnish, *c336*

Tears, 156

Technology, 546

communication and, 556–557

definition of, 551

effect of, 551

environment and, 554

food and, 554

health and, 552, *c553*

materials and, 552

medicine and, 554–555

recycling and, 553

of time measurement, 559

transportation systems and, 558–559

Velcro® and, 552

Technology in Science 33, 125, 161, 187

Teeth

human, *c153*

of machine, 472

Telecommunications, 546, *c557*

Telescopes, *c424*

Galileo and, 530

Hubble Space Telescope, *c536*

for looking at Sun, *c521*

Temperature

air pressure and, 188

effects on matter, *c334–c335*

graphing, *c204, 205*

vs. heat, 353

measuring, 194

solar energy effects on, 292

weathering and changes in, 264

Temperature scales, *c362,* 362–363

Terra **(satellite),** 202

Terraces, *c269*

Test Talk, 169, 305, 481, 569

Testing of matter, 319

Thales, 376, *c392*

Thermal energy, *p346,* 351, 353, *p353,* 354

Thermal Protection Materials and System Branch (NASA), 366

Thermogram, *p351*

Thermometer, *c352*

Threatened species, 120

Thunder, 375

Thunderstorms

cold front and, 192

hurricanes and, *c216,* 217, *c218*

tornadoes and, *c222,* 223

from tropical depression, *c216*

Time, 452–453

Timeline on use of lenses, *c424–c425*

Time measurement, 559

Tire recycling, *c296*

Tissues, *c8*

of human body, 143

of plants, 50

Tomato plant, 58

Topaz, 240

Topsoil, *c289*

Tornado, 210

compared to hurricane, 225

forecasting, 224, *p224*

formation of, *c222–c223*

hurricane and, *c218*

watches and warnings, 225

Torricelli, Evangelista, 194

TPS (Thermal Protection System) materials, 366

Trachea (windpipe), 148, *c149*

Tracking weather, *c196–c197*

Transcontinental jet service, *c559*

Transcontinental railroad, *c558*

Translucent, *p402,* 421

Transparent, *p402,* 421

Transpiration, *c51*

Transportation systems, *c558–c559*

Transverse waves, 408

Trees

climate information on, 198, *c198*

genus and, 12

as natural resource, 287

redwood, 47

stems of, *c51*

Triton (moon), 534, 535

Tropical depression, 210, *c216*

Tropical rain forests, 29, *c81*

Tropical storms, 215

names of, *c219*

stages of, 216

True bacteria, *c11*

Tsunamis, 273

Tuataras, 19

Tubelike vascular plant structures, *c14*

Credits

Illustrations

8-32 Marcel Laverdet; 9, 43, 49, 57 Robert Ulrich; 80-94, 184-198, 352-359 Bop Kayganich; 106-128, 189, 380-383, 408-410, 419, 442, 500 Peter Bollinger; 216-224, 288, 294 Tony Randazzo; 242-244, 264-272 Alan Male.

Photographs

Every effort has been made to secure permission and provide appropriate credit for photographic material. The publisher deeply regrets any omission and pledges to correct errors called to its attention in subsequent editions.

Unless otherwise acknowledged, all photographs are the property of Scott Foresman, a division of Pearson Education.

Photo locators denoted as follows: Top (T), Center (C), Bottom (B), Left (L), Right (R), Background (Bkgd).

Cover:

(T) ©Gerry Ellis/Minden Pictures, (C) ©Lynn Stone/Index Stock Imagery, (Bkgd) ©ThinkStock/SuperStock, (BL) Rubberball Productions.

Front Matter:

i ©Lynn Stone/Index Stock Imagery; ii ©DK Images; iii (TR) Getty Images, (BR) ©Royalty-Free/Corbis; v ©Jerry Young/DK Images; vi (TL) ©Zig Leszczynski/Animals Animals/Earth Scenes, (B) ©DK Images; vii Getty Images; viii (CL) ©Breck P. Kent/Animals Animals/Earth Scenes, (BL) ©E. R. Degginger/Color-Pic, Inc.; ix ©Dr. Dennis Kunkel/Visuals Unlimited; x (TL) ©Steve Wilkings/Corbis, (BR) Getty Images; xi (TR) Getty Images, (B) Stephen Oliver/©DK Images; xii (TL) ©Ted Mead/PhotoLibrary, (BL) ©Hubert Stadler/Corbis; xiii ©Alan Schein Photography/Corbis; xiv (TL) PhotoLibrary, (BL) ©Charles O'Rear/Corbis; xv Digital Vision; xvi (TL) Getty Images, (BL) ©Alan Schein Photography/Corbis; xvii ©Royalty-Free/Corbis, (BL) ©DK Images; xviii (TL) ©Paul & Lindamarie Ambrose/Getty Images, (BL) ©Stocktrek/Corbis; xix ©Yang Liu/Corbis; xxii ©Stephanie Maze/Corbis; xxiii (BC) ©Bill Varie/Corbis, (TR, CR) NASA, (BR) ©Scott T. Smith/Corbis; xxiv ©Richard T. Nowtiz/Corbis, Gallaudet University; xxv (CL) ©DK Images, (BL) Stephen Oliver/©DK Images, (TR) ©Dr. Ray Weil, University of Maryland, (CR, BR) NASA; xxvi ©Richard T. Nowitz/Corbis; xxviii (CC) Brand X Pictures, (CC, BC) Getty Images; xxix (L, CR, BR) Getty Images; xxx (BL, R) Getty Images, (TL) Brand X Pictures, (TC) ©Leonard Lessin/Peter Arnold, Inc.; xxxi (TL) Brand X Pictures, (BC) Getty Images, (BR) ©Jim Cummins/Getty Images.

Unit A:

Divider: (Bkgd) ©Tim Flach/Getty Images, (CC) Digital Vision; Chapter 1: 1 (Bkgd) ©Zig Leszczynski/Animals Animals/Earth Scenes, (CR) ©Richard LaVal/Animals Animals/Earth Scenes; 2 (BL) ©Ken Cole/Animals Animals/Earth Scenes, (T) ©Martha J. Powell/Visuals Unlimited, (B) ©DK Images; 3 ©Ralph A. Clevenger/Corbis; 5 (CR) ©Gusto Productions/SPL/Photo Researchers, Inc., (Bkgd) ©Martha J. Powell/Visuals Unlimited; 6 ©Martha J. Powell/Visuals Unlimited; 8 (BR) ©Eye of Science/Photo Researchers, Inc., (TL) ©Carolina Biological/Visuals Unlimited, (CL) ©SIU/Visuals Unlimited, (BL) ©Alfred Pasieka/Photo Researchers, Inc.; 10 (TL) ©Neil Fletcher & Matthew Ward/DK Images/Getty Images, (BL) Getty Images, (CL) ©Stephen Dalton/NHPA Limited; 11 (TL) ©T. Beveridge/Visuals Unlimited, (TL) ©L. Stannard/Photo Researchers, Inc., (CL) ©Eric Grave/Phototake, (BL) ©Ken Cole/Animals Animals/Earth Scenes, (BL) ©Craig Tuttle/Corbis, (CL) ©Royalty-Free/Corbis; 12 (CL) ©Ken Cole/Animals Animals/Earth Scenes, (BCL) Getty Images, (TL) ©DK Images, (BL) ©Kevin Schafer/Corbis; 13 (TR, TC, TCR, BR) ©DK Images, (TCL) ©Ken Cole/Animals Animals/Earth Scenes, (TC) ©John Conrad/Corbis, (TCR) ©Ray Richardson/Animals Animals/Earth Scenes; 14 (BL) ©John Durham/Photo Researchers, Inc., (L) Sue Atkinson/©DK Images; 15 (BL) ©DK Images, (TL) Karl Shone/©DK Images, (CL) Lee W. Wilcox; 16 (BL) ©Wolfgang Kaehler/Corbis, (TL) Getty Images, (CL) ©DK Images; 17 (BC) ©Larry Lee/Corbis, (CC) ©Steve Terrill/Corbis, (T) Getty Images; 18 (CR, BL, TCL) ©DK Images, (CL) ©Jane Burton/DK Images, (TL) Getty Images, (BCL) ©Ray Richardson/Animals Animals/Earth Scenes; 19 ©DK Images; 20 (TR) ©Jim Tuten/Animals Animals/Earth Scenes, (CL, BR) ©DK Images; 21 (TR, B) ©DK Images; 22 (BL) ©Philip James Corwin/Corbis, (TR) ©DK Images; 23 (BC) Jerry Young/©DK Images, (CL) ©Andrew Syred/Photo Researchers, Inc., (BR) ©F. J. Jackson/Robert Harding Picture Library, Ltd., (TR) Dave King/©DK Images; 24 ©Kevin Summers/Getty Images; 25 (TL, CR, CL) ©Dwight R. Kuhn, (TR) ©Chase Swift/Corbis; 26 ©DK Images; 27 (TR) ©John Conrad/Corbis, (TL) ©Peter Johnson/Corbis, (BR) ©Jeffrey L. Rotman/Peter Arnold, Inc., (Bkgd) ©Stephen Frink; 28 (TL, CL) ©Ray Richardson/Animals Animals/Earth Scenes, (BR) ©DK Images, (BL) ©E. R. Degginger/Color-Pic, Inc.; 29 (B) Digital Stock, (CC) ©DK Images; 30 ©Ray Richardson/Animals Animals/Earth Scenes; 31 (TL) ©Ken Cole/Animals Animals/Earth Scenes, (BL) ©Steve Kaufman/Corbis, (CL) ©Ralph A. Clevenger/Corbis; 32 (TR) ©Eric Baccega/Nature Picture Library, (B) ©Anup Shah/Nature Picture Library; 33 ©Manoj Shah/Getty Images; 34 (TL) ©Martin B. Withers/Frank Lane Picture Agency/Corbis, (CL, BL) ©DK Images, (CL) ImageState, (TR) ©Lonny Kalfus/Getty Images; 35 (TL) ©Martin B. Withers/Frank Lane Picture Agency/Corbis, (TL, BL, B) ©DK Images, (CL) ImageState; 36 (Bkgd) ©Patti Murry/Animals Animals/Earth Scenes, (BL) ©DK Images; 37 (CL, BL) ©DK Images, (BC) Getty Images, (CC) ©John Gerlach/Animals Animals/Earth Scenes, (BR) Jerry Young/©DK Images, (CR) ©Science VU/Visuals Unlimited, (TR) Brand X Pictures; 39 ©DK Images; 40 (Bkgd) ©M. P. Kahl/Photo Researchers, Inc., (TL) NASA; 41 (TCL) Getty Images, (Bkgd) PhotoLibrary; Chapter 2: 42 (B) ©Royalty-Free/Corbis, (T) ©George D. Lepp/Corbis; 43 (BR) ©Carolina Biological Supply Company/Phototake, (BL) ©John Kaprielian/Photo Researchers, Inc.; 45 ©George D. Lepp/Corbis; 46 ©George D. Lepp/Corbis; 48 (TL) ©DK Images, (R) ©TH Foto-Werbung/Photo Researchers, Inc.; 49 ©Dr. Jeremy Burgess/Photo Researchers, Inc.; 50 (TL, CR) ©DK Images; 51 (BR, TR) ©DK Images, (CR) Getty Images; 52 (TL, BR) ©DK Images, (TL) ©Gary Moss/Getty Images, (BC) Brand X Pictures; 53 (BC) ©Carolina Biological/Visuals Unlimited, (CR) ©DK Images; 54 (CL, B) ©Royalty-Free/Corbis, (TL) ©DK Images; 55 (TL) ©David Sieren/Visuals Unlimited, (TR) ©Owaki-Kulla/Corbis; 56 (TR) ©W. Treat Davidson/Photo Researchers, Inc., (TL) ©DK Images, (TL, B) ©Merlin Tuttle/BCI/Photo Researchers, Inc.; 57 ©John Kaprielian/Photo Researchers, Inc.; 58 (TL, CL, BL, BC, BR) ©DK Images; 59 (L, BC) ©DK Images; 60 (CL) Stephen Oliver/©DK Images, (TL, BL) ©DK Images; 61 ©Merlin Tuttle/BCI/Photo Researchers, Inc.; 62 (TL) ©Ed Reschke/Peter Arnold, Inc., (CL) ©Carolina Biological Supply Company/Phototake, (BL) ©John Shaw/Tom Stack & Associates, Inc., (TL) ©DK Images; 63 (Bkgd) ©Dwight R. Kuhn, (TR) Neil Fletcher and Matthew Ward/©DK Images; 64 Eric L. Heyer/Grant Heilman Photography, (BCR) Brand X Pictures, (BCL, R) ©DK Images; 65 ©DK Images; 66 ©Joseph Devenney/Getty Images; 68 (CL) Brand X Pictures, (BL) ©DK Images, (Bkgd) Digital Vision; 71 ©Royalty-Free/Corbis; 72 (Bkgd) ©Neale Clark/Robert Harding Picture Library, Ltd., (TL) NASA; 73 ©Breck P. Kent/Animals Animals/Earth Scenes; Chapter 3: 74 (T) ©Andrew Brown/Ecoscene/Corbis, (BR) ©George H. H. Huey/Corbis, (BL) ©Kennan Ward/Corbis, (T) ©Breck P. Kent/Animals Animals/Earth Scenes; 75 (BR) ©Raymond Gehman/Corbis, (TR) ©Raymond Gehman/NGS Image Collection, (BL) ©Jim Brandenburg/Minden Pictures; 77 ©Andrew Brown/Ecoscene/Corbis; 78 ©Andrew Brown/Ecoscene/Corbis; 80 (CL) ©Andrew Brown/Ecoscene/Corbis, (BL) ©David Keaton/Corbis; 81 (CR) ©Steve Terrill/Corbis, (TR) ©Michael Townsend/Getty Images, (BR) ©David Muench/Corbis; 82 (TL) ©Steve Kaufman/Corbis, (BL) ©Konrad Wothe/Minden Pictures; 83 (C) ©Raymond Gehman/NGS Image Collection, (BR) ©Steve Kaufman/Corbis, (T) ©George H. H. Huey/Corbis, (BC) Getty Images, (BL) ©Buddy Mays/Corbis, (TC) ©Daryl Balfour/Getty Images; 84 ©Biophoto Associates/Photo Researchers, Inc.; 85 (TR) ©Frank Lane Picture Agency/Corbis, (CR) ©Joe McDonald/Corbis, (TL) ©John Gerlach/Animals Animals/Earth Scenes, (CL) ©D. Robert & Lorri Franz/Corbis, (BR) ©DK Images, (TC) ©Tim Fitzharris/Minden Pictures, (BL) ©George H. H. Huey/Corbis; 86 (BL) ©Buddy Mays/Corbis, (BR) ©Jeff Foott/Nature Picture Library, (BC) ©John Cancalosi/Nature Picture Library; 87 ©Sally A. Morgan/Corbis; 88 (TR) ©Stephen J. Krasemann/DRK Photo, (CC, BR) ©Kennan Ward/Corbis, (CL) ©Michael Llewellyn/Getty Images; 89 (BL) ©Kevin Schafer/Corbis, (TC) Getty Images, (CL) ©Steve Kaufman/Corbis, (BR) ©Michael & Patricia Fogden/Corbis; 90 (TL) ©Roland Birke/Peter Arnold, Inc., (CL) ©Stephen Dalton/NHPA Limited; 91 (TL) ©Randy Wells/Getty Images, (BR) ©Ralph White/Corbis, (TR) Getty Images, (BL) ©Georgette Douwma/Getty Images; 92 (BC) British Antarctic Survey/SPL/Photo Researchers, Inc., (BR) ©Royalty-Free/Corbis, (TL) ©W. Perry Conway/Corbis, (BL) ©Roland Birke/Peter Arnold, Inc., (TC) ©Stephen Dalton/NHPA Limited; 93 (TR) ©Joe McDonald/Corbis, (TL) ©Royalty-Free/Corbis, (CL) ©George D. Lepp/Corbis; 95 ©Raymond Gehman/Corbis; 96 ©John & Eliza Forder/Getty Images; 98 (Bkgd) ©Neil McIntyre/Getty Images, (BL) ©D. Robert & Lorri Franz/Corbis; 101 ©DK Images; 102 ©Roger Ressmeyer/Corbis; 104 (BR) ©Alan G. Nelson/Animals Animals/Earth Scenes, (L) ©Tom Edwards/Animals Animals/Earth Scenes, (TL) ©George Rinhart/Corbis; 105 (Bkgd) ©E. R. Degginger/Color-Pic, Inc., (TR) ©Michael Fogden/Animals Animals/Earth Scenes; Chapter 4: 106 ©Orion Press/Corbis; 107 (TR) ©Frank Blackburn/Ecoscene/Corbis, (BL) ©Sullivan & Rogers/Bruce Coleman, Inc., (BR) ©Barbara Von Hoffmann/Animals Animals/Earth Scenes; 109 ©Orion Press/Corbis; 110 ©Orion Press/Corbis; 112 (CC) ©David Muench/Corbis, (TL, C) Getty Images, (BR) Hans Neleman/Getty Images; 113 (CC) ©Lynda Richardson/Corbis, (CL) ©Art Wolfe/Getty Images, (TCL, CR) ©DK Images, (TCR) ©Gary W. Carter/Corbis; 114 ©Royalty-Free/Corbis; 115 ©Ron Austing/Frank Lane Picture Agency/Corbis; 116 (BL) ©David Muench/Corbis, (R) ©Jon Sparks/Corbis; 117 (TR) ©Frank Blackburn/Ecoscene/Corbis, (BR) AP/Wide World Photos; 120 (CL) ©Sullivan & Rogers/Bruce Coleman, Inc., (BL) ©DK Images; 121 (CR) ©DK Images, (L) ©Barbara Von Hoffmann/Animals Animals/Earth Scenes, (BR) ©Peter Scoones/SPL/Photo Researchers, Inc.; 122 (BR) ©Martin B. Withers/Frank Lane Picture Agency/Corbis, (CL) ©1999 Tom Bean/DRK Photo, (CR) ©Marty Cordano/DRK Photo; 123 ©Marty Cordano/DRK Photo; 124 ©Bettmann/Corbis; 125 ©Bettmann/Corbis; 126 (B) ©Adrian Lyon/Getty Images, (CR) ©Vince Streano/Corbis; 127 ©Bruce Hands/Getty Images; 128 (CL) Getty Images, (BL) ©Doug Sokell/Visuals Unlimited; 129 (TR) ©Ed Reschke/Peter Arnold, Inc., (CR) ©Myrleen Ferguson Cate/PhotoEdit; 130 ©George Gerster/Photo Researchers, Inc.; 132 (Bkgd) ©Steve Allen/Getty Images, (Inset) ©Alain Choisnet/Getty Images; 135 ©DK Images; 136 (BL) NASA, (Bkgd) ©Jerry Driendl/Getty Images; 137 ©Dr. Dennis Kunkel/Visuals Unlimited; Chapter 5: 138 (BR) ©Dr. Kari Lounatmaa/Photo Researchers, Inc.; 139 ©Dr. Donald Fawcett & E. Shelton/Visuals Unlimited; 141 (L) ©Dr. Donald Fawcett/Visuals Unlimited, (BC) ©Dr. Richard Kessel & Dr. Randy Kardon/Tissues and Organs/Visuals Unlimited, (CR) ©Prof. P. Motta/Univ. "La Sapienza"/Photo Researchers, Inc.; 142 (L) ©Dr. Donald Fawcett/Visuals Unlimited, (BC) ©Dr. Richard Kessel & Dr. Randy Kardon/Tissues and Organs/Visuals Unlimited, (CR) ©Prof. P. Motta/Univ. "La Sapienza"/Photo Researchers, Inc.; 144 (BL) ©CNRI/Photo Researchers, Inc., (CL) ©Science Photo Library/Photo Researchers, Inc.; 147 (CR) ©SPL/Photo Researchers, Inc., (TR) ©Innerspace Imaging/Photo Researchers, Inc., (BR) ©Dr. Donald Fawcett/Visuals Unlimited; 152 ©Reuters/Corbis; 155 ©Alfred Pasieka/Photo Researchers, Inc.; 156 ©Prof. P. Motta/University "La Sapienza"/Photo Researchers, Inc.; 157 (TR) ©Susumu Nishinaga/Photo Researchers, Inc., (C) ©Dr. Fred Hossler/Visuals Unlimited; 158 ©Dr. Kari Lounatmaa/Photo Researchers, Inc.; 159 (CR) ©Science Source/Photo Researchers, Inc., (TL) ©Dr. David M. Phillips/Visuals Unlimited; 160 (TL, CL, BCL, BL) ©Bettmann/Corbis; 161 ©Dr. Donald Fawcett & E. Shelton/Visuals Unlimited; 162 Getty Images; 164 (B, Bkgd) ©Scott Camazine/Photo Researchers, Inc., (Bkgd) ©Dr. Wolf Fahrenbach/Visuals Unlimited, (BL) ©Tim Flach/Getty Images; 165 Getty Images; 168 (B) ©Bettmann/Corbis, (TR, BR) Corbis; 170 (T) ©Martha J. Powell/Visuals Unlimited, (TC) ©George D. Lepp/Corbis, (C) ©Andrew Brown/Ecoscene/Corbis, (BC) ©Orion Press/Corbis, (B) ©Dr. Richard Kessel & Dr. Randy Kardon/Tissues and Organs/Visuals Unlimited; 172 ©Daniel Zupanc/NHPA Limited; 176 (CC) Jerry Young/©DK Images, (CC) Steve Gorton and Gary Ombler/©DK Images, (Bkgd) ©Pat O'Hara/Corbis; 177 ©Steve Wilkings/Corbis.

Unit B:

Divider: (Bkgd) ©Alan Kearney/Getty Images, (CC) Brand X Pictures; Chapter 6: 178 (BR) Getty Images, (BR) ©DK Images, (TL) ©Earth Satellite Corporation/Photo Researchers, Inc.; 179 (CR) ©David Lees/Corbis, (BL) ©DK Images, (TR) Stephen Oliver/©DK Images; 181 ©Earth Satellite Corporation/Photo Researchers, Inc.; 182 ©Earth Satellite Corporation/Photo Researchers, Inc.; 184 ©Tom Van Sant/Corbis; 186 ©Charles O'Rear/Corbis; 188 (TR, CR) ©DK Images; 189 ©Darwin Wiggett/Corbis; 190 ©DK Images; 192 ©DK Images; 194 (L) ©David Lees/Corbis, (TR) ©Leonard Lessin/Peter Arnold, Inc., (BR) Getty Images; 195 (TR) Stephen Oliver/©DK Images, (BR) ©DK Images; 198 ©DK Images; 199 ©British Antarctic Survey/Photo Researchers, Inc.; 200 ©Mark Lewis/Getty Images; 202 ©Layne Kennedy/Corbis; 203 ©Jim Craigmyle/Corbis; 205 ©DK Images; 206 AP/Wide World Photos; 207 (BR) KSC/NASA, (Bkgd, BL) NASA; 208 (TL) Fritz Hoelzl/NOAA, (Bkgd) ©Jim Brandenburg/Minden Pictures; 209 (CL, Bkgd) Getty Images; Chapter 7: 210 (B) ©DK Images, (T) ©Reuters/Corbis; 211 (TR, CR) ©Japan Meteorological Agency, (BR, BL) ©Storm Productions, Inc.; 213 ©Reuters/Corbis; 214 ©Reuters/Corbis; 216 (BL, TL, CL, BR) ©Japan Meteorological Agency; 217 ©Adastra/Getty Images; 218 ©DK Images; 219 (CL) ©Cameron Davidson, (TL) ©Morton Beebe/Corbis; 220 (TL, BR) NASA, (BL) NASA/JPL; 222 (BL, BR) ©Storm Productions, Inc.; 223 (BL) ©Storm Productions, Inc., (CR) ©H. Hoflinger/FLPA-Images of Nature, (TR) ©ANT Photo Library/NHPA Limited; 224 (R) ©Reuters/Corbis, (CL) ©Jim Reed/Photo Researchers, Inc.; 228 (BC, Bkgd) Corbis; 231 NASA; 232 (BR) ©Chris Sattlberger/Photo Researchers, Inc., (TR) Albion Historian; 233 (Bkgd) ©Ted Mead/PhotoLibrary, (TC) ©DK Images; Chapter 8: 234 ©Adam Jones/Photo Researchers, Inc.; 235 (TC, TR, BL, CR, CC) ©DK Images, (BR) Richard M. Busch; 237 (CR) ©Judith Miller/©DK Images, (Bkgd) ©Adam Jones/Photo Researchers, Inc.; 238 ©Adam Jones/Photo Researchers, Inc.; 239 (TR, CR) ©DK Images, (BR) GeoScience Resources/American Geological Institute; 240 (BC, BCL, TR, BL, CL, TL) ©DK Images, (TL, BR) ©Colin Keates/Courtesy of the Natural History Museum, London/DK Images; 241 (CL) ©Colin Keates/Courtesy of the Natural History Museum, London/DK Images, (TL, TR, BR, BL, BC, CC) ©DK Images, (CL) Natural History Museum/©DK Images; 242 (TL, CL) ©DK Images; 243 (TR, BR) ©DK Images, (CR) Dave King/©DK Images; 244 (TR) Harry Taylor/Courtesy of the Natural History Museum, London/©DK Images, (TL, BR) ©Danny Lehman/Corbis; 246 (BL, CL, TL) ©DK Images; 247 (L) Alan Williams/©DK Images, (TR, TC) ©DK Images, (TL) Colin Keates/Courtesy of the Natural History Museum, London/©DK Images; 248 (TL, CL) ©DK Images, (TL, BL) Richard M. Busch; 252 ©Royalty-Free/Corbis; 253 Digital Vision, (TL) ©Bob Thomason/Getty Images, (TL) ©Barry Runk/Grant Heilman Photography, (TL) ©Andrew J. Martinez/Photo Researchers, Inc.; 255 Richard M. Busch; 256 (BL, BC, TL) JPL/NASA, (TR) NASA; 257 ©Hubert Stadler/Corbis; Chapter 9: 258 (T) ©Art Wolfe/Getty Images, (BR) ©Chris Reynolds and the BBC Team-Modelmakers/DK Images; 259 ©Jack Dykinga/Getty Images; 261 (CR) ©Owaki-Kulla/Corbis, (Bkgd) ©Art Wolfe/Getty Images; 262 ©Art Wolfe/Getty Images; 264 AP/Wide World Photos; 265 ©Jack Dykinga/Getty Images; 267 ©Owaki-Kulla/Corbis; 268 ©Paul A. Souders/Corbis; 269 (TR) ©Dave G. Houser/Corbis, (CR) ©Richard Bickel/Corbis; 270 ©Chris Reynolds and the BBC Team-Modelmakers/DK Images; 271 (TR, CR, BR) ©Gary Rosenquist; 273 (TL) ©George Hall/Corbis, (TL) Getty Images; 274 ©Roger Ressmeyer/Corbis; 276 (Bkgd) ©James Balog/Getty Images, (BR) ©Baron Wolman/Getty Images; 277 ©David Weintraub/Science Source/Photo Researchers, Inc.; 279 ©Chris Reynolds and the BBC Team-Modelmakers/DK Images; 280 (Bkgd) ©Ralph White/Corbis, (TL) NOAA; 281 ©Alan Schein Photography/Corbis; Chapter 10: 282 (T) ©Layne Kennedy/Corbis, (BR) ©Charles E. Rotkin/Corbis, (BL) ©Charles O'Rear/Corbis; 283 (CR) ©Kevin Burke/Getty Images, (BR) ©Owaki-Kulla/Corbis, (TR) Clive Streeter/©DK Images; 285 ©Layne Kennedy/Corbis; 286 ©Layne Kennedy/Corbis; 289 (R) ©Deborah Kopp/Visuals Unlimited, (TL) Clive Streeter/©DK Images, (TR) Jerry Young/©DK Images, (TC) ©DK Images; 290 (B) ©Sylvain Saustier/Corbis, (TC) ©DK Images, (CR) Colin Keates/Courtesy of the Natural History Museum, London/©DK Images, (TR) Andreas Einsiedel/©DK Images; 291 (TR) ©Robert van der Hilst/Corbis, (CR) Ivor Kerslake/The British Museum/©DK Images; 292 (TL) AP/Wide World Photos, (B) ©Kevin Burke/Getty Images; 293 (TR) ©Royalty-Free/Corbis, (CL) Corbis; 295 ©Charles E. Rotkin/Corbis; 296 (CR) Getty Images, (BC) ©Ricki Rosen/Saba/Corbis, (TR) ©Liz Hymans/Corbis, (TL) ©Owaki-Kulla/Corbis; 297 (B) ©Owaki-Kulla/Corbis, (TL) ©Carin Krasner/Corbis, (CL) ©DK Images; 298 ©Lucidio Studio, Inc./Corbis; 300 (Bkgd) ©Royalty-Free/Corbis, (BR, BC) Getty Images, (CC) ©Frederik Astier/Sygma/Corbis, (C) Brand X Pictures; 303 ©Kevin Burke/Getty Images; 304 (TL, BL) AP/Wide World Photos; 306(TL) ©Earth Satellite Corporation/Photo Researchers, Inc., (BCL) ©Adam Jones/Photo Researchers, Inc., (BL) ©Art Wolfe/Getty Images, (TCL) ©Sygma/Corbis; 307 (TR) Dave King/©DK Images, ©Layne Kennedy/Corbis; 309 ©Niall Benvie/Corbis; 312 (TC) Tom Ridley/©DK Images, (CC) ©DK Images, (Bkgd) ©Image Source Limited; 313 PhotoLibrary

Unit C:

Chapter 11: 314 (T) ©Kevin Schafer/Getty Images, (BL) ©DK Images; 315 ©Royalty-Free/Corbis; 317 ©Kevin Schafer/Getty Images; 318 ©Kevin Schafer/Getty Images; 320 ©Bernhard Edmaier/Photo Researchers, Inc.; 326 ©DK Images; 327 ©DK Images; 329 ©DK Images; 330 ©Hans Neleman/Getty Images; 335 (TR, CR, BR) Science Museum, London/©DK Images; 336 (R, BL) ©DK Images, (BL) Corbis, (CL) ©Royalty-Free/Corbis; 337 ©DK Images; 338 ©DK Images; 340 (R) ©Richard Megna/Fundamental Photographs, (Bkgd) ©Richard Laird/Getty Images, (B) ©Martin Keller/Getty Images; 343 ©DK Images; 344 (TL) JPL/NASA, (L) ©Cris Cordeiro/PhotoLibrary, (TL) Kennedy Space Center/NASA; 345 (CR) ©Royalty-Free/Corbis, (R) ©Charles O'Rear/Corbis; Chapter 12: 346 ©William Taufic/Corbis; 347 (BR) ©Chris Andrews Publications/Corbis, (BL) Stephen Oliver/©DK Images; 349 (CR) Getty Images, (Bkgd) ©William Taufic/Corbis; 350 ©William Taufic/Corbis; 351 ©A. Pasieka/Photo Researchers, Inc.; 352 Brand X Pictures; 355 (BR) ©Yann Arthus-Bertrand/Corbis, (CR) ©DK Images; 356 Stephen Oliver/©DK Images; 357 (C) ©Paul Seheult/Eye Ubiquitous/Corbis, (TR) ©DK Images; 358 (BL) ©Chris Andrews Publications/Corbis, (TR) ©Vera Storman/Getty Images; 360 ©Stone/Getty Images; 362 (B) Getty Images, (T) ©Christoph Burki/Getty Images; 363 ©Paul Seheult/Eye Ubiquitous/Corbis; 366 (Bkgd) ©Craig Aurness/Corbis, (BR) ©Mark Edwards/Peter Arnold, Inc.; 367 Corbis; 368 (BR) ©Bettmann/Corbis, (L) ©Stephen Simpson/Getty Images; 369 Digital Vision; Chapter 13: 370 ©Byron Aughenbaugh/Getty Images; 371 ©Cordelia Molloy/Photo Researchers, Inc., (TR) ©DK Images; 373 ©Byron Aughenbaugh/Getty Images; 374 ©Byron Aughenbaugh/Getty Images; 376 (R) ©DK Images, (BL) Clive Streeter/©DK Images; 378 ©Cameron/Corbis; 379 (BL) ©Richard Megna/Fundamental Photographs, (T) ©DK Images; 382 ©Cordelia Molloy/Photo Researchers, Inc.; 383 (TR, CR, BR) ©Loren Winters/Visuals Unlimited; 385 ©Kennan Ward/Corbis; 386 (BL, BR) Andy Crawford/©DK Images; 388 (BL, TR) ©DK Images; 389 Dave King/Courtesy of The Science Museum, London/©DK Images; 391 (TR) ©Sheila Terry/Photo Researchers, Inc., (TR) ©New York Public Library/Photo Researchers, Inc.; 392 (TL) ©George Bernard/Photo Researchers, Inc., (TC, CL) ©Science Photo Library/Photo Researchers, Inc., (BCL) The Granger Collection, NY, (CC) ©DK Images, (BL) Science & Society Picture Library; 393 (TL) Getty Images, (B) ©Royalty-Free/Corbis; 394 ©Jeremy Walker/Photo Researchers, Inc.; 396 Age Fotostock; 399 ©Cameron/Corbis; 400 (TL) The Granger Collection, NY, (CR) Getty Images, (BL) Age Fotostock; 401 (CC) ©Cooperphoto/Corbis, (CR) ©Cameron/Corbis, (Bkgd) Getty Images; Chapter 14: 402 ©NOAO/Photo Researchers, Inc.; 403 (BL, BR) ©DK Images, (TR) ©Southern Illinois University Biomedical Communications/Custom Medical Stock Photo; 405 (CR) Getty Images, (Bkgd) ©Spencer Jones/Getty Images; 406 ©Spencer Jones/Getty Images; 407 Getty Images; 413 (TL, BL) Getty Images, (CL) ©DK Images; 414 (TR, CR, BR) ©DK Images, (CR) Getty Images; 415 (CL) Getty Images, (TR) ©Bo Veisland, Mi & I/Photo Researchers, Inc.; 416 (BL) ©Chris Bjornberg/Photo Researchers, Inc.; (BR) ©DK Images; 417 (TL) The Science Musuem/©DK Images, (R) Mike Dunning/©DK Images; 418 (CR) Anthony Meshkinyar/Getty Images, (TL) ©Maxine Hall/Corbis; 419 (CR) ©Maxine Hall/Corbis, (L) ©Adina Tovy/Robert Harding Picture Library, Ltd.; 420 (BR) Andy Crawford/Courtesy of the Football Museum, Preston/©DK Images, (R) ©NOAO/Photo Researchers, Inc., (CR) Steve Gorton and Kari Shone/©DK Images; 422 (TL) ©Southern Illinois University Biomedical Communications/Custom Medical Stock Photo, (TL) ©David Parker/Photo Researchers, Inc.; 423 (Bkgd) ©David Parker/Photo Researchers, Inc., (CR) Getty Images; 424 (TR, CR) ©E. R. Degginger/Color-Pic, Inc., (BL) Dave King/Courtesy of The Science Museum, London/©DK Images, (BCL) Peter Anderson/Courtesy of Saxon Village Crafts, Battle, East Sussex/©DK Images, (BC) ©DK Images, (BR) National Maritime Museum /©DK Images; 425 (CL) Getty Images, (TR) ©Matthew Borkoski/Index Stock Imagery, (BCL) ©Bettmann/Corbis, (BL, BCR) ©Science Photo Library/Photo Researchers, Inc., (BR) Dave King/Courtesy of The Science Museum, London/©DK Images; 428 (CL) ©Steve Taylor/Getty Images, (BL) Getty Images, (BL, CL) AP/Wide World Photos, (Bkgd) ©Ulf Wallin/Getty Images; 429 (L) Corbis, (CL) ©Alan Smith/Getty Images; 429 AP/Wide World Photos; 431 ©DK Images; 432 (B, Bkgd) ©Royalty-Free/Corbis; 433 ©Alan Schein Photography/Corbis; Chapter 15: 434 (T) ©Scott T. Smith/Corbis, (BL) ©Robin Smith/Getty Images, (BR) ©Bill Bachmann/PhotoEdit; 435 (TL) ©DK Images, (TR) ©Jim Craigmyle/Corbis, (BR) ©Michael S. Lewis/Corbis; 437 ©Scott T. Smith/Corbis; 438 ©Scott T. Smith/Corbis; 439 Getty Images; 440 (TCL) ©Jim Craigmyle/Corbis, (CL) ©Tom & Dee Ann McCarthy/Corbis, (TL) ©Robin Smith/Getty Images, (BL) ©Raymond

Gehman/Corbis; 441 ©Robin Smith/Getty Image; 442 ©DK Images; 443 (C) Jane Burton/©DK Images, (TR) ©DK Images; 444 (TL, B) ©Bill Bachmann/PhotoEdit; 445 ©Stanley R. Shoneman/Omni-Photo Communications, Inc.; 446 (BL) ©World Perspectives/Getty Images, (TR, TL) ©DK Images; 447 (TL) ©Bettmann/Corbis, (R) ©DK Images; 448 (BR) ©Michael S. Lewis/Corbis, (TL) ©John Lund/Getty Images, (TL) ©Royalty-Free/Corbis; 449 ©Royalty-Free/Corbis, (BR) Jane Burton/©DK Images, (BR) ©Bettmann/Corbis, (BR) ©Peter Langone/Getty Images; 450 ©FotoKIA/Index Stock Imagery; 452 ©Lester Lefkowitz/Corbis; 453 ©Connie Ricca/Corbis; 455 Jane Burton/©DK Images; 456 (BL, BR, TL) NASA; 457 ©Royalty-Free/Corbis; Chapter 16: 458 (T) Digital Vision, (BL) ©DK Images, (BR) ©DK Images; 459 ©Lester Lefkowitz/Corbis; 461 (CR) ©Bob Krist/Corbis, (Bkgd) Digital Vision; 462 Digital Vision; 464 (CL, BL, TL) ©DK Images; 465 (TR, BR, CR) ©DK Images, (Bkgd) Getty Images; 466 (TR, TL) Getty Images, (CR) ©Tony Freeman/PhotoEdit, (CR) Brand X Pictures, (BR) Andy Crawford/©DK Images; 467 (TR) ©DK Images, ©Paul Almasy/Corbis, (Bkgd) ©James P. Blair; 468 ©Lester Lefkowitz/Corbis; 469 (T) Peter Arnold, Inc., (B) Getty Images; 470 (BL) ©DK Images, (R) ©Joe McBride/Getty Images, (CC) Getty Images; 471 (CR) ©DK Images, (C) ©DK Images, (TR) ©David Vaughan/Photo Researchers, Inc., (CL) Brand X Pictures, (CL, BL) Getty Images; 472 (C) Corbis, (TL) Getty Images; 473 (TR) ©DK Images, (TL, BL) Getty Images, (BL) Brand X Pictures; 474 ©Jeff Greenberg/Index Stock Imagery; 476 (Bkgd) ©John Noltner/Aurora Photos ©Keith Pritchard/Alamy Images; 478 ©Royalty-Free/Corbis, (BR) Philip Gatward/©DK Images, (CR) Steve Gorton and Gary Ombler/©DK Images, (BC) Getty Images, (BCR) ©DK Images, (BR) ©Fukuhara, Inc./Corbis; 479 ©DK Images; 480 (BR) ©Hulton-Deutsch Collection/Corbis, (Bkgd) ©Alan Towse/Ecoscene/Corbis; 482 (TL) ©Kevin Schafer/Getty Images, (TCL) ©William Taufic/Corbis, (CL) ©Byron Aughenbaugh/Getty Images, (BCL) ©Spencer Jones/Getty Images, (BL) ©Scott T. Smith/Corbis; 483 Digital Vision; 484 ©Steven E. Frishling/Sygma/Corbis; 488 (TC) Stephen Oliver/©DK Images, (Bkgd) Getty Images, (Bkgd) ©Paul & Lindamarie Ambrose/Getty Images.

Unit D:

Divider: (Bkgd) NASA; Chapter 17: 490 ©Mark Garlick/Photo Researchers, Inc.; 491 (BL) ©Adrian Neal/Getty Images, (BR) Royal Greenwich Observatory/©DK Images; 493 (CR) GSFC/NASA, (Bkgd) ©David Parker/Photo Researchers, Inc.; 494 ©David Parker/Photo Researchers, Inc.; 496 ©John Sanford/Photo Researchers, Inc.; 498 (B) ©Arnulf Husmo/Getty Images, (TL) ©John Sanford/Photo Researchers, Inc.; 500 ©John Sanford/Photo Researchers, Inc.; 501 ©John Sanford/Photo Researchers, Inc.; 502 (B) ©Mark Garlick/Photo Researchers, Inc., (Bkgd) ©David Nunuk/Photo Researchers, Inc., (TL) ©John Sanford/Photo Researchers, Inc.; 503 (CL) ©G. Antonio Milani/Photo Researchers, Inc., (TL) ©Adrian Neal/Getty Images, (BR) ©David Parker/Photo Researchers, Inc., (CC) ©Mark Garlick/Photo Researchers, Inc., (Bkgd) ©Magrath Photography/Photo Researchers, Inc.; 504 (TR) Royal Greenwich Observatory/©DK Images, (TL) ©John Sanford/Photo Researchers, Inc.; 505 (CL) Royal Greenwich Observatory/©DK Images, (TR) ©Roger Ressmeyer/Corbis; 508 ©Galen Rowell/Corbis; 511 ©G. Antonio Milani/Photo Researchers, Inc.; 512 (CL) NASA, (Bkgd) ©Fotopic/Index Stock Imagery; 513 ©Stocktrek/Corbis; Chapter 18: 514 (T) ©A. Morton/Photo Researchers, Inc., (B) ©USGS/Photo Researchers, Inc.; 515 (BR) Getty Images, (BL) JPL/NASA; 517 (CR) ©Bettmann/Corbis, (Bkgd) ©A. Morton/Photo Researchers, Inc.; 518 ©A. Morton/Photo Researchers, Inc.; 520 ©NASA/Photo Researchers, Inc.; 522 (TR) ©USGS/Photo Researchers, Inc., (TL) JPL/NASA; 523 JPL/NASA; 524 (CC, TR, TL) Getty Images; 525 JSC/NASA; 526 (TR) U.S. Geological Survey, (Bkgd) (TL) JPL/NASA; 527 JPL/NASA; 528 (BR) JPL/NASA, (TL, CR) NASA; 529 (TL) Getty Images, (CL, BL) NASA, (CC) JPL/NASA; 530 (CL) ©Scala/Art Resource, NY, (TL) JPL/NASA; 531 (T, BR) JPL/NASA, (BL, CC, BC, BR) ©Calvin Hamilton Solar Views, (BC) NASA; 532 (TL, Bkgd) ©Mark Garlick/Photo Researchers, Inc.; 533 JPL/NASA (B, TR) ©Mark Garlick/Photo Researchers, Inc.; 534 (L) JPL/NASA, (CR) ©NASA/Roger Ressmeyer/Corbis; 535 (TL) ©James King-Holmes/Photo Researchers, Inc., (CR) ©NASA/Photo Researchers, Inc.; 536 (TL) ©Bettmann/Corbis, (BC) ©NASA/Corbis, (BR) JPL/NASA, (TR) NASA; 537 (BL) ©Mark Garlick/Photo Researchers, Inc., (BL) Jet Propulsion Laboratory/NASA Image Exchange; 540 (CL) ©USGS/Photo Researchers, Inc., (CL, BL) JPL/NASA, (CL, BL) Getty Images, (BL) ©Comstock Inc., (BL) NASA, (Bkgd) ©Royalty-Free/Corbis; 542 ©Mark Garlick/Photo Researchers, Inc.; 543 JPL/NASA; 544 (TL) The Granger Collection, NY, (BL) Jim Ballard/Getty Images; 545 (TR) ©Royalty-Free/Corbis, (Bkgd) ©Yang Liu/Corbis; Chapter 19: 546 (T) ©Tibor Bognar/Corbis, (BR) ©DK Images; 547 Getty Images; 549 (CR) ©Stevie Grand/Photo Researchers, Inc., (Bkgd) ©Tibor Bognar/Corbis; 550 (Bkgd) ©Tibor Bognar/Corbis, (BR) ©Ted Soqui/Corbis; 552 (BL) ©J. Burgess/Photo Researchers, Inc.; 552 (TL) ©Donald Specker/Animals Animals/Earth Scenes, (CR) Getty Images; 553 Getty Images; 554 (BR) ©Simon Jauncey/Getty Images, (TL) ©Stevie Grand/Photo Researchers, Inc., (TC) ©Ted Horowitz/Corbis; 555 (L) ©Matt Meadows/Peter Arnold, Inc., (CR) ©James King-Holmes/Photo Researchers, Inc.; 556 (CR) ©DK Images, (R) Dave King/©DK Images, (TL) ©David Young-Wolff/PhotoEdit; 557 (CR) Getty Images, (TR) ©Courtesy of the Museum of the Moving Image, London/©DK Images, (TL) Tina Chambers/Courtesy of the National Maritime Museum, London/©DK Images, (TL) ©DK Images; 558 (CC, CR, CL, BL) ©Bettmann/Corbis, (BL) ©Archive Holdings, Inc./Getty Images, (BL) George H. Huey Photography, Inc.; 559 (CC) ©Museum of Flight/Corbis, (CR) Getty Images, (BR) ©Claro Cortes IV/Reuters/Corbis, (BC) ©Reuters/Corbis, (BL) Dave King/Courtesy of the Science Museum, London/©DK Images; 560 ©Chuck Swartzell/Visuals Unlimited; 562 (Bkgd) ©Roger Ball/Corbis, (BL) ©General Motors Corp. used with permission, GM Media Archives, (BR) Hughes Electronics Corporation; 565 ©David Young-Wolff/PhotoEdit; 566 (R, L) JPL/NASA; 567 (TL) GRIN/NASA Image Exchange, (CR) MSFC/NASA, (BR) Hubble Heritage Team/NASA; 568 (TL) The African American Registry®, (Bkgd) Getty Images, (CL) Medtronic, Inc.; 570 (L) ©David Parker/Photo Researchers, Inc., (CL) ©A. Morton/Photo Researchers, Inc., (BL) ©Tibor Bognar/Corbis; 576 (BC) Mike Dunning/©DK Images, (Bkgd) NASA.

End Sheets:
©Steve Bloom Images/Alamy Images.

EC CRU 10 9 8 7 6 5 4 3 2 1

EM32